THE CHIC DIET

The Dietary & Psychological Tactics Of The Urban Elite

Kit Olsen

Wunderland Press
New York, NY 10020

ISBN-13: 9781494979485
ISBN-10: 1494979489

First Edition
14 13 12 11 10 / 10 9 8 7 6 5 4 3 2 1

Printed in the United States of America

TABLE of CONTENTS

UM, IT'S NOT A FAD... IT'S A LIFESTYLE

HIDE IT, BETCH

I'M PRETTY SURE THAT'S ILLEGAL

FODDER FOR YOUR SHRINK

ALL THAT OTHER CRAY SHIT

BYEEEEEEEEEEE

FOREWORD

The chic girl is something of an enigma. Girls either hate every last ounce of her soul or want to be her best friend. Boys are either enthralled or repulsed by her. Her doctor is concerned for her, yet wants to know all of her tips and tricks. The sales staff at Barneys fucking loves her. Bathroom attendants loathe her. Everywhere she goes, people simply turn and stare. Who, oh who, is that incarnation of chicness? She is captivating yet despicable, attractive yet controversial, beautiful yet monstrous. Simply put, she is fabulous.

Everyone knows that a chic girl has more issues than Vogue, but who cares? She's obvi something of a thin guru. People always want to know how the chic girl maintains her glamorously gaunt figure. How does she get her arms so thin? Her stomach is so tiny! Does she do Bikram yoga? Is she a flexitarian? Vegetarian? Vegan? I saw her holding a green juice—does she cleanse? What does she eat for breakfast?

Unfortunately for the adoring public, chic girls are notoriously selfish and discreet. She will simply mumble something about grilled chicken breasts or Pilates before quickly changing the subject. No matter how hard others press, she will never divulge her svelteness-inducing secrets. But guess what? I will.

I'm here to dispel all of your preconceived notions of the chic elite's dietary, social and cultural habits. Her bumbling response of "a combination of a balanced diet and exercise" is, well, a big fat lie. I really don't think that half a pack of Marlboro Lights, an Adderall and a soy cappuccino from Starbucks constitutes a balanced meal. In all truthfulness, the chic girl is a cray ol' betch, and her diet and exercise regimen mirror that *completely*.

I know that it might be, like, gauche of me to spill the secrets of my chic brethren, but the rest of the world has a right to know. So I've gone ahead and compiled a really long list of some tactics that I have observed my friends and colleagues employ in order to lose weight. And I'm, like, a really good source because I went to a super legit fashion school *and* I did a bunch of internships at really fancy places. Basically, I've gotten bitched at by a ton of *totally* chic people, many of whom I have observed starving, weeping and doing all of the things that I describe in this book.

Just so you know, this book is *totally* just FYI and is completely satirical. Like, I just want to make you laugh, or something. No one should take any of this to heart or use it as some sort of handbook for turning into a cray psychotic betch. Like, I really love the people in my life, but they're kind of terrible. I mean, they're obvi unhinged and their habits should *definitely* not be emulated. Plus, no one could actually accomplish all of the things listed, as some tactics completely contradict some others.

Or maybe you would just become, like, the ultimate chic girl. She is, after all, a super fake, manipulative, lying and uptight sociopath. But she has really cute Prada shoes. And a super hot Saint Laurent bag. And, like, really skinny legs. Then again, maybe that's all that matters, right?

THE FUNDAMENTALS

Cigarettes

Every girl living in New York City knows that cigarettes are chic. They help stave off hunger, they draw the eyes to your pretty new Tom Ford lipstick and they totally complete your outfit, whatever the hell you may be wearing. They add a new dimension to your perfume and precede your arrival with an aromatic cloud that announces, “CHIC IS ON ITS WAY”.

They let people know that you work in fashion/PR/ marketing/advertising or that you’re an artist and/or writer. How effortlessly chic is that? They pair excellently with both black Americanos or Diet Coke, bringing out bitter tasting notes that dance on your tastebuds. Not only that, you get double chic points for pairing them at the same time. Nothing says "chic" like a white knuckled-fist clenching onto a zero-calorie beverage while the other hand is showcasing the timeless cigarette.

Cigarettes have come a long way fashion-wise, too. Take Sobranie Cocktail 100's, for example. They are the epitome of young and fun chicness, what with the vibrant array of pastel choices in each box. You can match your cigarette to your outfit or even your mood. So symbolic. And the gold foil lining? Um, yes, please. Their Slims are cute too, if you're still into that whole ombre trend. But if you can't get your hands on these brightly colored novelties, it's not the end of the world. You can still look just as polished with a simple Marlboro Ultra Light or, if you're uber progressive, an electronic Blu cig. You'll look like a really fashion-forward robot.

Now, think back on any chic girl who ever graced this planet. Every one of them smoked. It's just, like, a part of initiation into the Chic Girl's Club. I mean, Audrey Hepburn, Edie Sedgwick, Jane Birkin, Françoise Hardy... come on. And, like, every single it-girl today is perpetually gripping a cigarette. Go to any reasonably fashionable soirée and it's like walking into the smoking lounge at Charles de Gaulle. *Très enchantée, non*?

Plus, check out any random photo of off-duty models. What do they always seem to be holding onto, other than the handles of their gorg handbags? That's right—cigarettes. I mean, isn't it obvi? Smoking is just, like, a really great alternative to eating. It can quell hunger pains in a snap and it totally keeps your calorie hungry-hands and mouth busy. And all for no carbs!

Feeling hungry? Puff on a Marlboro Light. Upset? You can bum one of mine. Out of Klonopin? Here, let me light that for you.

So while all of your friends are busy talking shit about your outfit or seducing your boyfriend behind your back, the ever-so-classy cigarette will always be there for you. Loyal, skinny and dependable. What more could you ask for?

CAFFEINE

Caffeine, like, totally speeds up your metabolism, didn't you know? Plus, it's a great accessory. Nothing says chic better than a cup from Starbucks or Dean & Deluca in the wee early hours of the morning when you're looking haggard and/or frumpled on your way to work or, even better, fashion school. An un-labeled white paper cup from some obscure-yet-still-hip coffeehouse works too.

If you're going to go iced, make sure that you get a black-on-black beverage. Half-and-half just screams plebeian. Toting a clear cup filled with dark and bitter liquid, on the other flawlessly manicured hand, shows the world that you're not one to let calories fuck with you. Opaque cups allow you the luxury of surreptitiously indulging in a latte, so choose accordingly. Get a Venti or XXXXL size if you really want to express your general indifference to letting solid foods take up space in your petite stomach. Egg white omelette? I think not. Bonus points if the cup is taller than the length of your face.

No matter what, do not succumb to cheap coffee. One who spends $5 on good coffee is one who is not wasting money on Pret A Manger sandwiches, and everyone totally knows that. But carrying around a cup from Dunkin or, God forbid, a fucking bodega, is like screaming to the world, "I JUST INHALED A JELLY DONUT

AND/OR TACO AND I DON'T CARE WHO KNOWS." Tsk tsk. No shame. If you really must, and you really shouldn't, chug that shit in a dark, feces-splattered alley and walk away discreetly. AND ABSOLUTELY NO THERMOSES. Chic girls don't make their own shit—they pay other people to do so. Duh.

Coffee breath? Never heard of it. Waifs in the know floss obsessively and chew gum all day long to prevent themselves from partaking in the unbeseeming act of chewing their breakfasts, lunches or dinners. If you're really hungry, you can have a green juice, you undisciplined cow. As for staining? You really should only be using either Marvis or Theodent toothpaste, both of which have proven track records for fighting cigarette and coffee tinging and are, like, really expensive. Like, *Barneys* sells Marvis. Duane Reade Colgate just isn't very chic.

Cigarettes and coffee go hand-in-hand, didn't you know? They're, like, two birds of a F/W13 Christopher Kane feather dress. Feel free to take liberty in pairing them as often as you'd like (and it should be often). The two will soon prove themselves to be worthy weapons in your arsenal against appetite.

So, like, cheers. Lift up your 20 oz. cup and let the empty void that is your alimentary tract be filled with calorie-free glory. Those on benzos should feel free to have two.

Diet Coke

"Feed me!" your rumbly tumbly cries out as it enters its 11th hour of neglect. You continue to ignore its pleas until you coolly reply, "Here, have some Diet Coke." The pathetic creature quietly whimpers until it can no longer be heard, its protests silenced by the delicate melody of effervescent chicness.

Styled by the likes of Lagerfeld, Gaultier and Jacobs, hoarded by prepubescent Eastern European runway models, uh, everywhere, and toted by the endless stream of catty PR girls dressed like death come alive, the throat-prickling ambrosial beverage is ubiquitous in chic social circles. Like, the ads have featured Coco Rocha and Ginta effin' Lapina. C'mon.

Zero guilt for the oh-so-satisfying hit of cloyingly sweet goodness that you've been denying yourself in the form of actual food? Sweet. Oh, so it might cause cancer or heart disease? Um, that's not going to happen until, like, a lot later though, right? Oh. Well, it tastes, like, *really* good. I'm sure it's totally fine!

Plus, it will fill that whiny complaining baby that is your gut and make it shut the fuck up. Having bubbles fill your tummy is a lot chicer than having a Shack Stack or even Energy Kitchen stuffed in there. Bubbles! How cute.

It’s also super moderate in its caffeine content. I think. Like, if you took too many Adderalls, or whatever, and can’t handle a coffee, you can totally just have a Diet Coke instead. See? Heart attack averted. Lifesaver!

Oh, and Diet Pepsi. Don't get me started on Diet Pepsi! The marketing team at Pepsi Co. may believe that blitzkrieging the fashionable zombies at NYFW with an incessant parade of free cans might sway their loyalties, but the Ohmigod-how-adorbs-obsession over the matching Jonathan Adler straws faded as soon as the tents came down. Speaking of which, can you pass me my Diet Coke back, please?

If you have a maje case of orthorexia, you can spring for Coke Zero, or fucking Zevia. Those are made with Splenda or Stevia, which are both totally amazing inventions. More on those later. They taste totally different though, and neither pairs as well with Marlboro Lights as Diet Coke, either. But there’s no point in arguing semantics. Diet Coke is just the best, you know? What can I say—I’m a purist.

ADDERALL

Ohmigod, swoon. This might possibly be the greatest psychopharmaceutical gift that the diet gods have ever bestowed upon us. Or just the one that every chic person, well, *ever* really, really likes. It just makes any interest in eating go away while turning you into a better, more efficient version of yourself. My friend, Ally, told me that Wellbutrin killed her appetite but, like, I don't really feel like I'm ready to give up smoking yet. My hand would be so bored.

Anyway, extended release is totally the way to go. They keep you consistently medicated (i.e. not hungry) all day long and come in really pretty capsules. They're just really chic. Think Hermès orange or that really pretty turquoise blue that was everywhere a few seasons ago. Some are even colorblocked! Yeah yeah, colorblocking's *so* two seasons ago—we get it. But pharmaceutical manufacturers aren't really extolled for keeping with current fashion trends, you know? Plus, they're not as tacky as Xanax. Monogramming is *so* over.

What? You don't have a prescription? Oh. Just traipse on over to any psychiatrist on the UES and totally spaz out. He'll be like, "How are you feeling?" and you'll be like, "Huh?" Then he'll tut-tut and ask, "Have you had problems concentrating in the past?" *Cue silence.* "What?" you will ask with glossy eyes. "Oh dear," he will say as he pretends to care. "Sorry," you will then squeak out adorably while giving your best *oopsies* shoulder shrug. *Scribble scribble* and you've got yourself some Schedule II self-control.

There are some caveats, but of course. You shouldn't mix Adderall with five cups of iced coffee unless you want to have an anxiety attack in the middle of the street, which is so not chic. Public displays of neuroses aren't cute, even if you're really skinny and wearing an Isabel Marant dress. It's also going to give you severe dry mouth, but this is actually a blessing in disguise. Your skin will become super hydrated when you glug down all of that lemon water to compensate, and you won't be as bloated. Yay.

Cigarettes are also amazing on Adderall, like you're smoking on a fluffy cloud. Just delectable. You also become, like, really talkative and friendly, so you can make lots of friends on your 45-minute long smoking breaks. And *everyone* knows that talking burns calories. It's, like, science.

Ambien

Sleep is great for, like, regenerating your worn-down body and resetting your energy levels. As long as you get the proper amount, your skin looks better and you're not as bloated as Lindsay's post-Radiesse-ed face, either. But do you know what else it is simply excellent for? Not eating.

When you're asleep, you can't reach for the bag of Cooler Ranch Doritos that you have hidden in the back of your oven for impromptu end-of-the-line binge sessions. Sleep is an escape from the real world, a period of time during which calorie and carb counts are not endlessly scrolling through your brain like the fucking Matrix. It is, essentially, a time for dietary peace and very much needed relaxation.

But what if your hands and heart are still shaky from the excessive amounts of X, Y and Z stimulants with which you bombarded your body over the course of the day? Crawling into bed while in this state will just worsen any anxiety that might be lingering in your zany little head, causing you to unnecessarily focus on your breathing and heart rate while pondering your life choices. It's like a sad little downward spiral into cray-land as you rock yourself back and forth in your literal cuckoo's nest.

Cue: Ambien. Or Lunesta or Sonata or Seconal (oooh, so vintage) or even a Benadryl. It's like a fuzzy cashmere blanket in an amber bottle. Pop one and you'll soon succumb to warm, cuddly feelings, sporadic bouts of giggles and creepy Glen Bishop-esque smiling as your blanket swallows you up in its silky embrace. You will then be whisked off to a state of konked-out blackness in which calories can never hurt you.

Plus, you really need sleep to maximize your weight loss ability. Like, it's super important to get enough shut-eye in order to regulate your metabolism and appetite. Sleep deprivation is linked to increases in cravings for carbs (gasp) and susceptibility to obesity (ew). Getting eight hours (or more!) is optimal, since that's the only way that your levels for two super important hormones will be kept in check. Yes, even if you snort up two Ritalins. Leptin is totes necessary to inhibit your appetite and energy expenditure when you're awake. And then there's this other one called gremlin, or something, that does the complete opposite and turns you into a nasty little fatty. Can you guess which one gets pumped out by the bucketload when you're sleepy?

Should Ambien be your sleep med of choice, get your bony ass to bed soon after popping one. If you decide to "have a little fun" with it, you must live with the fact that you likely raided every nook and cranny of your kitchen, though you will have no recollection of it the next day. The only evidence of your binge will be the empty popcorn bags and pillaged takeout containers strewn across your floor. Do not, I repeat, do not fuck around with Ambien. Just take it and Go. To. Sleep.

So if you're feeling like a ravenous bridge troll who is on the verge of devouring anything and everything edible in its path, stop and take an Ambien. The disgruntled ogre within you will soon be overcome with euphoria as she traipses through a dreamy land that is void of hunger and self-indulgence. Food will be the last thing on your mind, trust me. It's like the antidote for being a fat fuck. And no need to take a handful—you're not Neely O'Hara.

Artificial Sweeteners

Every chic girl will have her sweetener of choice that she will stick to like religion. There are, of course, some girls who just don't give a fuck and will use any white powder (No, not that one! Okay, that one too. But more on that later!) that is touted as being zero-calorie. Yup, even including aspartame and saccharin. Have fun nursing your tumors later on, bitches.

The vast majority of skinny young things will refuse to use anything other than sucralose (Splenda) because "it's made from real sugar, duh". The orthorexics and those girls who wear a lot of Free People and Winter Kate will swear by stevia since it's, like, all natural. Which it is. I think.

Healthier-than-thou idiots will chirp incessantly about the agave nectar, lavender honey, brown rice syrup or faux sugar runoff that was used to naturally sweeten their gluten-free bran muffins, but they are just sad and misinformed bobbleheads who are wildly unaware of their slowly expanding thighs. THOSE ARE ALL JUST FANCY DISGUISES FOR SUGAR A.K.A. CELLULITE. Like, didn't you know that agave nectar is just refined sugar parading around in Isabel Marant? Ohmigod, you didn't? Well, you learned something new. Make sure not to fall victim to the wily white minx's deceit and temptation, as she can be a tricky little betch.

But back to our real friends. Artificial sweeteners are invaluable to chic girls during the darkest of times. They provide a ray of hope during low carb dieting and help to quell sweet teeth and prevent hypoglycemia-induced binges. They lay the foundations for diet beverages and low calorie snacks, much to the gratefulness of the starved waifs that are wandering aimlessly around the city. And just a sprinkle brings a sense of palatability to otherwise deplorable snacks like grapefruit or unsweetened chocolate almond milk.

And where would we be without our skinny Cinnamon Dolce lattes or Lily's dark chocolate bars? Don't even get me started on our undying need for diet sodas and Vitamin Water Zeroes. In spite of all of the health problems that may arise from using these gifts from the laboratory gods, the daily presence of artificial sweeteners is a necessary evil in the life of a chic girl. I mean, just mention the term "sugar-free" and they will saunter over in numbers to check out the goods.

But caution and skepticism should always be high when approaching anything that is labeled as being "sugar-free". Any girl who has ever binged on sugar-free candy knows very well to steer clear of maltitol, the ultimate ravager of bowels. Everyone has to experience the aftermath of inhaling an entire bag of sugar-free Dove chocolates to know that you should never again consume anything for which maltitol is the first listed ingredients, lest you WANT to look like the poster child for protein deficiency in Ethiopia.

So the following are your take home messages. Pick your

poison and stick with it, because that's the closest to actual sugar that you'll be getting for a long, long time. Avoid “natural sweeteners” like the plague, unless there's a big fat ZERO printed alongside the Total Carbohydrate count. And always err on the side of caution when dealing with all things “sugar free”, i.e. don't pull an Augustus Gloop—gluttony is *SO* not cute.

Chewing Gum

One way to take your spacey mind off of food is to keep your mouth occupied. But not in, like, a slutty way, you know? So when you're not busy inhaling a trillion chemicals, popping pills or guzzling down some sort of hunger-drowning beverage, chew some sugar-free gum. Teeth cleaning *and* appetite slaying? Double[mint] yay.

There are *sooo* many different flavors out that, like, you'll never really need to eat any actual dessert. I mean, why ingest thousands of calories and grams of carbs when you can just chew a 5-calorie stick of gum and indulge in the whole experience? It's all very Violet Beauregarde, but without all of the bloating and humiliation.

Extra recently came out with all of these cray flavors that actually taste freakishly like apple pie, mint chocolate chip ice cream, rainbow sherbert, lemon squares, orange creamsicles, root beer floats and strawberry shortcake. They're kind of gross, but still really good at the same time. One annoying thing about this line is that the packaging is garish, but it's still not as bad as, like, Bubble Yum or, God forbid, Big League Chew.

There are always the classics, like Juicy Fruit and Big Red, both of which are nice departures from the 427 varieties of mint flavors that are available. Honestly, I can't really tell the difference between any of the minty ones except that some are in the blue (peppermint, yum) family and some are of the green (spearmint, ew) variety. Aside from flavor, I prefer blue-hued gums because the packaging is more appealing. Emerald doesn't really go with my skin tone.

Speaking of which, the chicest gum packaging award goes to 5 Gum, right? The black is so sick. But I can never tell what the fuck flavor I'm buying, so I'm always in for a surprise. But whatever. Even if you don't like a flavor, it's not like it lasts long anyway. Which is why turnover is crucial. Chic girls are all about asking each other if they want gum and "Ohmigod, yes" agreeing in unison every ten minutes. They all need something to help moisten their Adderall-inflicted cottonmouths, right?

In the same vein as Marlboro Lights, you go through, like, a pack a day anyway. And at 5-calories a stick, you're getting a really good dietary deal. If you're really hungry, you can swallow it—it doesn't actually stay inside of you for seven years. Trust me, I Googled it. And you're, like, totally burning calories when you chew. It's like low intensity steady state cardio for your mouth. Plus, it helps to mask coffee stink and that weird sweet-smelling breath that you get when you haven't consumed food in over 10 hours. *Such* a multi-tasker.

I don't know what I would do without gum, especially when I'm all strung out and about to grind my teeth down into oblivion. It's just a necessary lifesaver that keeps your mouth busy, quells cravings for sweets, freshens your breath and tones down the many signs of a mild eating disorder. It's like gum and chicness are a match made in heaven. You *do* know that's why there's a designated pocket shaped exactly like a pack of gum in every designer handbag, right?

Sparkling Water

Perrier, Pellegrino, Ty Nant and Voss, with the occasional Gerolsteiner or Hildon thrown in. It might sound like a Kanye West song about carbonated water, but those listed are the ones to order when you're dehydrated. Maybe Bling H2O too, if you can convince someone to pay the $50 for it while they're drunk. There are fucking *rhinestones* on the bottle; how cutesy is that?

Some places have cray fancy bottles like Lurisia or other obscure brands with names that are impossible to pronounce, so order those whenever you can. You will seem well-traveled and *très chic*, and your tablemates will fidget uncomfortably as they Google "Saint-Géron" under the table to make sure that you didn't just order a bottle of vintage French chardonnay.

Bubbly water is a godsend for hunger pains, much in the same way that Diet Coke can help take the edge off when your stomach decides to do its best impersonation of a dying whale. Not only that, it is an excellent way to fill your stomach before a meal. Pound a few cups of the fizzy stuff before digging in to your seared Branzino, and you'll realize that you're full after eating only a fraction of what you would normally ingurgitate. It's like an ephemeral version of fiber that won't sit around and threaten you with the risk of imminent flatulence.

And have you ever *been* to a fashion event? Those bitches serve nothing *but* sparkling water, Diet Whatever and champagne. You couldn't find a bottle or glass of still water if you tried. And do you know *why*? Ugh. Obvi you haven't been paying attention. Let me reiterate—it's just really practical, not to mention uber stylish. Like, did you know that there's a water fountain in Paris that dispenses sparkling mineral water? Um, swoon. Leave it to the French.

Trust me, fizzy water is great because it's full of minerals and doesn't contribute to cellulite. Some people, unfortunately, can't stomach it, especially if they're on, like, Topamax. My other roommate, Lauren, manipulates her doctor into giving her piles of the stuff for her imaginary migraines, and now she weighs, like, 89 pounds. But I tried it once and my Diet Coke tasted like tepid vomit, so I vowed never to take it again. So I guess if you're on medication that causes carbonated cups of heaven to taste like shit, then you have no choice but to drink Fiji, Evian, Acqua Panna, Smart Water, or even Volvic. But under no circumstances should you be drinking Poland fucking Spring, okay? You're not a peasant.

CHAMPAGNE

Alcohol is a daily, and sometimes hourly, fixture in the life of the chic girl, which is kind of ironic considering how caloric it is. But what can we say? It's a necessary evil. There really isn't a better way to *tszuj* up your life in moments of dire need other than, maybe, Vyvanse. Or cocaine. Or a molly. Or whatever. Anyway, it has seemingly magical powers, giving you the ability to accomplish unfeasible tasks without so much as a second thought. Like, even a few sips can give you a 67% less neurotic thought process, which makes you a lot more likable, apparently. A glass (or four) during your chic power lunch can make the harrowing task of heading back to the office seem somewhat intriguing and, daresay, fun. It's also great for dulling the agonizing pain of having to endure interactions with dull and/or unpleasant people, both of whom always seem to flock to you in droves. Sigh. Such is the life of a chic girl.

Anyway, back to the important matter on hand—calories. If you're not careful, you can end up ballooning into a Baby Beluga, which, contrary to popular belief, is not as cute as you'd think. So while that basil gimlet might *sound* uber yum, please refrain yourself before a sad little man in a garish yellow nylon jacket comes running over with a harpoon. Um, I don't *care* if pre-bloat Betty Draper drank them. She also made fucking pot roasts and named her baby EUGENE. Don't even get me started on the Band-Aid.

Ugh. So, where were we? Ah, yes, our dear frenemy, the sugar-infused cocktail. She will promise you a whirlwind of fun for your unassuming tastebuds, only to abandon you once it's all over with the hefty tab of 328 calories. Don't. Just don't. You must resist, even when the "libations menu", what with its pretentious descriptions of house-made tinctures typed out oh-so-authentically in Baskerville Old Face font, tries to woo you with its siren song. “Would you like to see the cocktail menu?” the model-slash-bartender will ask with what you're sure is a hint of challenge in his voice. “No,” you will respond coolly. “Just a glass of Dom P Rosé.“

What is chicer than champers? Nothing. Everyone knows that. That's why $50 pours or $2,000 bottles of liquid chic are omnipresent wheresoever you may choose to imbibe, be it at brunch or at those Wall Street bros' table. And, at less than a hundred calories per glass, you can indulge in as many as you'd like, so long as you were behaving like a good drunkorexic earlier that day. It's not like you really *need* food anyway, unless you're one of those girls who morphs into the Abominable Snowman after sipping (chic girls never *knock* or *pound*) a few and requires greasy gastrointestinal padding. Like its non-alcoholic siblings, sparkling water and diet soda, a continuous flow of bubbly can help to fill the empty void that is your stomach after quite the harrowing day. Did someone say 24-hour Champagne Diet?

There's, like, a lot of variety too. Dom Perignon is, of course, *always* there, glowing and leering at you as it spews out sparkler detritus all over your *steak et oeufs*. The label is in *cursive* too, so how much chicer could it get? Moët, Perrier-JouËt and Veuve make their occasional appearances when someone is feeling cheap. Krug and Cristal if they're feeling fancy. I'm also really digging the copper latticing on the Beau Joie right now—it's very Hervé Léger S/S13.

I can't really tell the difference, but everyone says that their favorite is Ace of Spades, so I'm going to say that too. I think it's just because each bottle is, like, obscenely expensive and gaudy, but still possesses that touch of glamour that only money can buy. Plus, Beyonce and Gwyneth drink it. So, yea.

If you're feeling maj ano, you can order some Laurent-Perrier Ultra Brut. There are only, like, 60 calories in each serving. It's Kate Moss's favorite, natch. Plus, my friend, Melissa, says all of the 15-year old models drink it. She walked in some obscure show for an "indie" designer and did two presentations last Fashion Week, so I totes believe her.

Another uber important lesson that I will so graciously bestow upon you (what would you do without me?)—Cava and Prosecco *so* do not qualify as champagne, so please don't refer to them as such. You will come off as uber *déclassé* and everyone will discuss your ignorance in audible whispers. Yes, they are all sparkling wines, but the prestigious bestowal of the title "Champagne" only applies to bubbly stuff that is produced using grapes from the Champagne region of France.

Ohmigod, can't you just feel yourself becoming *way* more cultured the more you listen to me? I should totes look into becoming the go-to sommelier for all of the fashionistas below 14th Street, *non*? Maybe I will open a speakeasy-cum-*enoteca* on the LES that serves strictly seasonal fare, such as endangered ramps with lavender-scented truffled honey burrata. I will be the young and hip proprietor who mingles amicably with her adoring patrons, enrobed in Theysken's Theory and dripping in Dominic Jones. When I'm feeling particularly francophilic, I will serve a dry Bordeaux in a vintage Breton top and opaque stockings with my Lanvin flats, à la everyone's favorite thinspo, Alexa Chung. Chic overload, I DIE. Hm, maybe I can pitch the idea to Melissa's sugar daddy.

But I digress (again). If you want to revel in some ethanol-derived fun, make sure that your choices are wise. Should you not be in a champagne kind of mood, opt for a Belvedere soda or glass of Merlot. Just don't be *that* girl who orders red wine in a club. Ew. And while that garishly pink-hued, black sesame-infused cocktail with the oh-so-cute name sounds totes amaze, exercise some self-control. The repercussions otherwise will ripple through your conscience and epidermal layer for eternity, not to mention *totally* kick you out of ketosis. Not cool.

THE MECHANICS

Overdigestion

If you simply *must* partake in the consumption of solid food, you should, at the very least, make sure to grind every last morsel down into oblivion. Failure to do so will likely result in an uber bloated belly, which could be mistaken for (insert gasp here) obesity.

Now, as you may have figured out, many chic girls are not comfortable with ingesting anything other than caffeinated beverages or bright green magma. But, sometimes, a situation arises in which one must eat a salad or, God forbid, an actual entree. When this type of undesirable event transpires, one must utilize every type of digestive tool available in order to convert said vittles into the chic elite's favored physical state—liquid.

As unattractive as it may be, mastication is key. Chew that shit up like there's no tomorrow. The more that you break food up in your mouth, the less work that your innocent little stomach has to do. Plus, if you take a really long time to chew every bite, everyone else will finish their food before you and won't notice that you've barely touched the contents of your own plate. Their hypotheses about your suspected eating disorder will also be grossly invalidated. I mean, you had food in your mouth the entire time!

Chewing supposedly helps you to eat less too, since satiety

signals, or whatever, are normally sent to your brain at a snail's pace. By taking longer to chew, you'll realize when you're actually full before committing the disgusting act of overeating. Kind of irrelevant, since it's not like chic girls are ever really hungry anyway, what with all of the appetite suppressants coursing through their veins and blobs of fiber and bubbles filling their tummies. But for those of you who like to go *au naturel* by eschewing Adderall and Phentermine (um, why?) this can be an effective weight loss tool.

Making sure to chew food thoroughly is, in itself, common knowledge. Belly fat abolitionists, on the other hand, are known to always go the extra mile. Such overachievers, aren't we? Anyway, this is where digestive enzymes come in. Sure, you chewed all of that nasty food up into a molten state, but what now? I mean, there's still the possibility of gas formation (ew) and ineffective digestion by your own stomach acid and pancreatic enzymes.

Like, did you know that, for every 10 years that you age, your pancreas produces less and less enzymes? You can't even get Botox for your pancreas to make it stop being old, or whatever, either. It's really sad. But if you take supplemental digestive enzymes, they'll help to pick up the slack. It seems like there's a medication for all of our inadequacies these days. We live in a really great world.

So, I usually use the Simple Digestive Formula from Whole Foods because I read that Rachel Roy uses it and everyone knows that she's really chic. Plus, it's from Whole Foods, so yea. There are, like, 7 different enzymes in there, but I don't know what they are since I never took a formal Biology class in college. But I'm sure that they're really great. Anyway, these pills also have ginger and turmeric in them, which I know for a fact are really good for you because Organic Avenue sells shots of them for $4 each. Like, what a steal, right? It says on the label to take one with each meal, but I usually take a handful. You can never be too efficient, you know?

My boho chic friend, Ally, buys this really New Age-y brand for, like, $50 a bottle, but that is just, like, totes unnecessary. I mean, I don't think that designer enzymes are a "thing". Whatever your pick, the bottles are not cute or iconic in the way that Duane Reade prescription bottles are, so this is a great excuse for you to pick up a really sick pill case from Tiffany or Henri Bendel. I recommend the Elsa Peretti Thumbprint. It's, like, really classic.

BEING COLD

"I am fuh-reezing!" must be one of the most overheard phrases within chic social circles. So commonplace, in fact, that the chattering of teeth and rattling of bones have really just become ambient noise. Of course, when you are sporting a flimsy Alice by Temperley dress with opaque tights (just *adorable*, by the way) in mid-February with a body fat percentage in the single digits, having your organs shake violently is to be expected. But what the overweight do not know is that waifs everywhere intentionally aspire to be frigid at all times, both literally and figuratively.

Like, did you know that you can burn up to 400 calories per hour *just* by shivering? Well, if you didn't, then you're welcome. And if you're standing adorably in some winter wonderland, your body can burn up to 10% additional calories while attempting to warm both your goosebump-adorned skin and the icy air that enters your lungs. Ohmigod, it's like a free SoulCycle session, but without all of the sweat, Diplo and cringeworthy affirmations.

You can take baby steps on your journey down the rungs of the thermometer by simply wearing minimal amounts of clothing during the colder months. From there, you can slowly work on becoming a colder person by sleeping without a blanket and/or with your window open at night. A lot of my friends don't use their heaters in the winter too, both to stay shivery and to save money for new Rachel Comey boots. What can I say? We're just really good at multi-tasking.

Other ways of hobnobbing with Jack Frost include sucking on ice cubes for snacks, chain smoking on your freezing cold fire escape in little to nothing and going for 5 AM jogs through Central Park. There's even a company that makes these exercise shorts with compartments for ice packs, but they're not very flattering or cute. Um, I think I'll just stick to my Lululemon.

You can, as with everything else, take this weight-loss tactic to the extreme by submerging your entire body into a bathtub full of ice cubes or swimming in subarctic water. I bet that your fat would atrophy like cray and just disintegrate off, like with CoolSculpting, that uber expensive freezing procedure that's all the rage in plastic surgeons' offices around the city. I know that there's a group that swims in the ocean off of Coney Island in the wintertime, but, I mean, who wants to go to Coney Island? Ew. Just take a cold shower instead.

Whatever your chosen method of low-temperature torture might be, your shivering endeavors will not be for naught. It's been scientifically proven that cold temperatures have prolonged effects on raising metabolism, even after your body is warmed up after exposure. You'll definitely quiver some fat off and, let's face it, you'll look really cute in the process, what with your flushed cheeks and red-tipped nose. And when people ask, "What blush are you wearing? Nars? Giorgio Armani?" you can give them a bewildered look and say, "Oh, no! That's just my natural glow." *So* chic.

Diuretics

Nothing is worse than waking up in the morning looking like the titular character from Georges Méliès' *Le Voyage dans la Lune.* It just ruins your entire day and hurdles you into a bottomless pit of frustration, wallowing and regret. Why, oh why, did you have to have that palmful of Utz chips yesterday? What's wrong with you? Have you no self-control?

There never was, is, or will be any situation in which bloating could be considered cute. And once it decides to grace you with its presence, it's close to impossible to get it to leave. No amount of intense cardio, skin slapping or ice pack-ing will get the pooled swelling to vanish in a reasonable amount of time. Think of it as one of those B&T party crashers who ruin all of your photos with their Forever 21 rompers and unpleasant vibes. *So* not desirable.

While it's difficult to completely eliminate bloat once it's arrived, there are ways to mitigate and prevent its presence. One such method is to go and get a lymphatic drainage massage, during which a therapist will vigorously paw at your face and body while cooing out holistic voodoo nonsense. If you're not in the mood for shelling out hundreds of dollars to inhale lavender fumes while being lectured on why you simply *must* try Reiki healing, you can opt for diuretics instead. Think of them as laxatives for your bladder.

A lot of your favorite necessities, such as caffeinated drinks and Adderall, are also diuretic in nature, hence the dizzying continuum of trips to the bathroom. But if those aren't cutting it and your cankles are *still* uber swollen, you can always supplement with some targeted formulas. There's always good ol' Diurex or those generic "water pills" with the seemingly DIY-ed labels. None of them are magic bullets, however, and will usually take at least a day to get rid of a substantial amount of bloat. But they're good for diuretic-loading beforehand when you know that there's an important event coming up at which you simply must appear ASAP (As Shriveled As Possible). Remember, skinniness is all about prevention and perseverance.

For those aliens who are not pill poppers, you can go the more natural, albeit less effective, route of drinking special herbal teas. This is likely what your yoga instructor would recommend that you do. Most of these blends will contain fennel, uva ursi and dandelion, or whatever organic herb *du jour*. Just peruse the tea aisle and pick one out on your next hours-long Nutrition Label-examining excursion through Whole Foods. Gaia Herbs' offering is unflatteringly entitled "Gas & Bloating", so head to the checkstand with the least attractive female store clerk for minimal judgment and embarrassment should you choose to go with that one.

If you are diligent in your distension-banishing ways, prepare to be rewarded with a flat belly and taut skin. Honestly, as long as you stick with the tried-and-true combination of sparkling water,

Adderall and no salt, like, ever, you should be fine. But for those dark and shameful days on which you must deal with the aftermath of gorging on prosciutto the night before, have a box of diuretics on standby if you don't want to look like the poster child for Grave's Disease upon waking. Your neck line will thank you.

FIBER

As un-chic as it may be, girls who strive for skeletal status are obsessed with bowel movements. Like, OBSESSED in that all-consuming Ohmigod-why-haven't-I-gone-to-the-bathroom-yet-my-belly-is-going-to-explode-I-must-get-my-claws-on-some-All-Bran-STAT kind of way.

Wheat bran, oat bran, psyllium husks, Metamucil, Benefiber, glucomannan, flax seed meal, chia seeds... you name it, we've binged on it. Not only is fiber a useful method for, well, moving things along, it also helps to make us feel so full that we don't want to eat. Um, a non-pharmaceutical appetite suppressant? Yes, please.

Take my roommate, for example. She really isn't very fond of eating, so she mixes Benefiber and chia seeds into every liquid she consumes so that she doesn't get hungry. Come to think of it, the only things that I really see her eat are Scandinavian bran crisps slathered in sugar-free grape jelly or salsa. And everyone knows that those compacted discs of sawdust just pass right through you and comes out the other end looking exactly the same as they went in. Her colon must be sparkling clean. So jelly.

Like I said, the chic elite are engrossed in what plops into the toilet. Groups of girls will discuss which fiber supplements they're taking, what helps them to go No.2 more easily and which laxatives work best, all the while silently competing over how many quality bowel movements they have daily. Don't believe me? You're obvi not in the know. Go and eavesdrop on that gaggle of pretty young things over there. See? Told you so.

When you're not eating carbs, or anything much in general, digestive elimination is important. Plus, it makes your stomach flatter. Any girl who's just expelled an impressive nasty will immediately run over to the mirror to check out how much her stomach has depressed. She might even hop on the scale afterward to see if there was any impact there, as well. It's just, like, chic girl nature.

Which is why fiber is uber important and is always on our minds. Like when you check the nutrition label on anything you eat ever, it's one of the first things that you check. ESPECIALLY since you can subtract it from the total number of carbs, the #1 enemy of chic girls everywhere.

People are always talking about how fashion models eat weird shit like facial tissues, cotton balls and Paper Source wrapping paper so that they don't feel full, but that's just dumb and *totally* unnecessary. I guess it's because they pull those kids out of school when they're, like, thirteen. They just don't know any better. Which is sad, really, because I'm sure that even sugar-free berry Metamucil tastes a lot better than antibacterial Kleenex.

So, like, let's toast to fiber, our dietary BFF, with some Benefiber vodkas. We can totes take a trip to the bathroom together later.

Laxatives

Um, why does every New York Times article about models' diets, like, EVER mention how Ex-Lax is flying off of shelves during fashion week? Who really takes Ex-Lax anymore? It was a staple in the arsenals of chic girls in the days of yore, but there are, like, SO many better options in modern times.

Let's face it—Ex-Lax hurts and the brand is synonymous with overweight, constipated commoners. I mean, if you're going to go the Duane Reade pill popping route, Dulcolax is where it's at. The tablets are sooo adorable and tiny, and they work without giving you debilitating cramps that make you collapse on the cold bathroom tiles. MiraLAX is a good choice too, but it's hard to get down and the taste and smell are reminiscent of plastic poison. And the glass bottles of Magnesium Citrate are for when you mean business. If you keep the lemon-lime flavored ones in the fridge, they can be slightly more palatable when coupled with a straw, tasting like really salty Sprite. Anyway, that one will help to blow out whatever the hell may have been resting in your digestive tract—it is definitely not for the faint of heart.

All of the above mentioned draw water INTO the colon to gently facilitate the elimination process, as opposed to rattling the fuck out of it so that every last solid molecule comes out. There will be a whole lot of gurgling, but no cramps! Yay.

Some girls swear by Ballerina tea, but that shit is the same as seeping a fistful of Ex-Lax in some hot water. Sorry, but I don't enjoy waking in the middle of the night in a cold sweat, kicking my feet and curling my toes as I clench my stomach and rue the moment that I imbibed in that cruel, cruel liquid. I refuse to drink that or Smooth Move unless I have a steady supply of Ambien or Tylenol PM nearby, and I advise that you do the same.

There are definitely some great all-natural alternatives out there too. Namaste-ing hippies love to preach about aloe, burdock and herbal formulations, all of which can be great so long as you don't go overboard. The main thing to watch out for is senna, which is the main ingredient in the aforementioned evil entities that are Ex-Lax and Ballerina tea. Since most herbal formulas suggest that you take, like, eight pills at a time anyway, you can adjust the dosage to your needs accordingly.

But what can I say—I'm a colon moisturizer, as opposed to a bowel shaker. I guess I'm just more gentle like that. Whatever your choice, digestive catharsis is a go. You just have to be careful with the latter, since your bowels can pretty much stop functioning properly without them over time. And while some forms of substance abuse MIGHT be glamorous, laxative dependence is SO not.

Colonics

"Have you ever had one of these before?" the colon hydrotherapist (such a chic title for what she actually does) will ask in a soothing voice as she unwraps what is basically a back-door dildo and its accompanying tubes from the sterile packaging. "Oh, yes," the chic girl will reply as she tries to mitigate the double chin that forms as she attempts to look over from where she is subconsciously lying on her back. "All the time."

When the trifecta of solid food abstinence, fiber supplementation and laxative abuse just isn't cutting it, colon hydrotherapy is an effective, forceful solution. It's also great if you need to look really skinny ASAP. One of the hydrotherapists told me that one colonic is equivalent to having, like, seventeen bowel movements in an hour, which no amount of bran could ever accomplish. It's like gastrointestinal wizardry.

Anyway, the colon hydrotherapist will lube up that THING and have you help her guide it up your YOU KNOW, as if it were a totally normal occurrence. Then you will proceed to make small talk as she kneads the shit out of your colon. The whole process is kind of demeaning, but watching everything that flows through that illuminated box is sort of magical. The fact that there's a tube shoved far up your nether regions will slip your mind as you alternate between squeaking out that the-pressure-is-too-much-and-could-she-please-release-it and being entranced by what comes out once she does.

Trying not to watch the disgusting outflow is sort of pointless, since, like I said, chic girls are obsessed with their bowels. Your eyes will be glued to that viewing chamber like some coprophilic poovert. But it's okay. I mean, that's what you're there for. You're just concerned for your digestive health, right?

It's just really annoying because you have to go get waxed before your appointment so you don't come off as some sort of hippie cavewoman. And it's really, insanely expensive after tipping. But such is the life of the urban elite.

And, of course, after that final bathroom visit before you leave, you will inspect the flatness of your stomach from all angles. Was it worth it? Um, yes, you decide as you skip on over to the front desk to book your next appointment. Yes it was.

I'M JUST TRYING TO BE HEALTHY

Juice Cleansing

"I just love it so much," the chic girl will say as she digs through her giant Saint Laurent tote to produce that oh-so-familiar blue-capped bottle of despair. "It makes me feel *sooo* good. I can, like, drink this everyday." Her friends will all nod knowingly as they pull out their own bottles of trendy green juice. They will all fight back their cringes as they take ladylike sips, being careful to avoid green mustaches, and fill the air around them with resounding "Ohmigod yum"s.

Nobody other than yoga instructors or panda bears will ever willingly choose a concoction of kale, parsley and spinach fluid over BonChon chicken, but chic girls will never admit that. To everyone in their social network, and basically anyone who will listen, they will worship green juice since it provides them with *sooo* much energy and *sooo* many nutrients. But honestly? They just love to cleanse because it's basically socially acceptable anorexia.

Not eating anything at all can raise some red flags, but how could anyone judge you when you're constantly glugging down gallons of vitamins and minerals? You're just really concerned about your health, you know? Plus, it'll make everyone else feel terrible about their own eating habits, which means bonus points for you. Every chic girl is at least a little bit (i.e. very) supercilious and loves to be on the receiving end of an envious glance.

And if subsisting on green water for hours on end is what it takes to avoid looking like a Triceratops in that Opening Ceremony dress, then so be it. Besides, it's not like it's all work and no play. There's always that throat-raping lemonade and oh-so-glorious cashew milk to look forward to, right?

Try not to go overboard with the regimen, though. The company sends you *way* more than necessary, so you don't have to drink them all. A day's supply contains, like, more than 1,000 calories, which is *way* more than what chic girls are used to eating. And, by stretching the juices out, you can totes turn a 3-day cleanse into a weeklong one. Talk about being frugal, right?

If you've endured so many Blueprint cleanses that you're O-VER-IT, then you can always go for Organic Avenue. The orange is cute, I guess. I don't think they got the memo that Pantone Orange is kind of last season, but whatever. A lot of people *swear* by Juice Press, but the labels are *so* not cute. I love their gazpacho juice, but my only aversion is to the typographic clutter that cloaks each bottle. They really need to hire someone to re-do their branding. Don't they know that part of the point of juice cleansing is to be seen carrying around a chic bottle?

But juicing really *can* be enjoyable, I guess. There are times when I do actually enjoy my Green Coco juice and think to myself,

"Wow, I could really do this everyday." But then I'll see a pastrami sandwich and it's game over. Not that I would ever eat a pastrami sandwich, of course. *That* would just be a mia episode waiting to happen.

Gluten Sensitivity

"Ohmigod, so I totally just found out that I have, like, gluten sensitivity," every chic girl ever will announce to her friends at a minimum of one point in her life. She didn't actually find out shit, but knows that making an official declaration of this gastrointestinal misfortune will allow her to openly refuse wheat (a.k.a. most carbs) at all future meals without sounding like the annoying girl with the borderline eating disorder that she really is. That way, she'll *have* to stick to her perpetual nemesis, the low carb diet. Or at least in public. *So* clever and brilliant, right?

"You mean Celiac Disease? I read about that in the Times," the token wannabe-cerebral acquaintance will chime in as she flips her perfectly Brazilian Blown-out hair and shoots back a thinly-veiled expression of doubt.

"Um, no," chic girl will respond while fighting the urge to roll her eyes. "But I still get, like, *really* debilitating digestive issues. It's *so* unfair. You wouldn't understand since you don't have it. You're *so* lucky." Bitch.

Keen skeptics will question the validity of these supposed 'Doctor's orders', but who cares, right? The truly chic know that gluten is a no-no and that it should be avoided at all costs. I mean, bread used to be for *peasants*. But being that girl who *never* eats bread or pasta or dessert instantly makes you uber annoying and hateable. All of your pastry-eschewing efforts will be for naught as your frumpier frenemies make bitter comments like "of course she's skinny—she never eats" or "I would be like that too if I subsisted on Diet Coke and Marlboro Lights" while shoveling Payard croissants into their Lip Tar-adorned mouths.

But nobody would ever rag on someone for having, like, a disease, you know? While it's totes acceptable to talk shit on friends with terrible psychological relationships with food, doing so about those with supposed medical disorders, real or not, is *so* uncouth. I mean, it's just really not nice.

Proclaiming gluten sensitivity is, simply put, a really strategic move for the modern day chic girl—it forces her to keep to her diet in order to save face, while protecting her from being on the receiving end of a verbal stoning from jelly peers. It's a great excuse to be able to exercise anorexic tendencies in public, but with a totally legitimate reason.

So, yea. That bread looks a-ma-zing, but I really can't have any. It's so sad. Oh, you can't have it either? How come? Ohmigod, you're sensitive to gluten too? Twinsieeees.

DETOXING

If there is one event that every chic girl dreads, it is that moment in which she has no choice but to pick up that loathsome pair of "fat jeans" that had been exiled to the back of her closet. Size 26? She might as well be wearing a muu-muu.

While slow and steady weight gain can be ignored in the short-term via the strategic utilization of maxi skirts and control top leggings, there comes a time when addressing the topics of muffin tops and chafing thighs can no longer be avoided. Desperate times call for desperate measures, which is where every chic girl's favorite pastime comes in.

There are varying degrees of severity to detoxing, and the relative intensity of the path that a girl chooses to take is directly proportional to how mentally unstable she is. But, as has been seen with all other lifestyle and dietary choices, the extremely unhinged are usually the skinniest and chicest girls around. Take my sample sized roommate, Sydney, for example. Bitch never, ever, ever eats real food and actually throws a manic bipolar-esque fit if you try to hand her a bowl of braised kale. She is perpetually detoxing. But she looks *so* good in busy prints *à la* Clover Canyon, which is definitely something that you can't say about just anybody. So, like, totally *quod erat demonstratum*, you know?

The mere utterance of the phrase, "I'm *cleansing*," is all that it takes for members of a chic circle to nod their heads in compassion and understanding. The practical girls will choose to partake in sensible diets of organic vegetables and fruit, all the while cutting out "toxic" necessities such as caffeine, alcohol and tobacco. I guess that's the prim and proper route to take, but it all just seems so slow and uneventful. Plus, why the need to withhold our much-needed drugs, coffee and cigarettes? It's not like the purpose of detoxing is to reap the health benefits or to rid yourself of chemicals. We *want* to err on the side of sickness, but without actually being sick, you know? Like, haven't you been on Tumblr lately? Sunken cheeks and eyes are so hot right now.

Now, juice cleansing falls within the wide range of techniques used for detoxing, but there are so many other options. There's the Master Cleanse, which everyone who hasn't been living under a rock is familiar with. If you decide to go that route, I suggest that you sweeten your lemon firewater with Splenda or stevia instead of calorific maple syrup. You'll lose a lot more weight since you're not ingesting, like, 100 grams of sugar a day from the unnecessary addition of sugarific tree tappings. You could also just drink green smoothies, which will at least give you a bit of fiber. There are a bajillion different kits available at Vitamin Shoppe, too, if you can handle the heaping scoops of powdered detox shakes or handfuls of horse pills.

If you're uber serious about major detoxing and even more

maj weight loss, just do a water fast. Religious people do it for weeks, or even months! Doctors always warn that it's dangerous, but I don't think so. I mean, Sydney's doing it all of the time. Come to think of it, maybe she's just really spiritual and I just never really understood her. You guys, now I just feel really bad.

Anyway, whatever your chosen method may be, stick to it! If you really lack self-control, you can book yourself a trip to one of those luxe “detox spas” in California, Thailand or Italy. Basically, you just pay thousands of dollars to have a team of doctors, nutritionists, masseuses and estheticians starve you for a week. But they starve you in a really posh setting with back-to-back sessions of a chic girl's favorite things, like facials, lymphatic massages, colonics and light yoga, so you barely notice your hunger. Apparently, Kate Moss and Gwyneth are regulars, so no extra explanation is necessary.

Don't have an extra three thousand bucks lying around? You can be resourceful and do what my roommates and I did during Hurricane Sandy—an obligated water fast. All we did was clear out the shelf of sparkling water at Trader Joe's and march straight back home, with nary a package of food in hand. Everyone was going crazy and scrambling for the cases of Poland Spring, but we were like, “Um, no.” If we were going to do a water fast, we were going to do it right, you know? And then we stayed indoors for, like, three days, painting our nails and reading old issues of fashion magazines. It was pretty successful, since each of us lost a few pounds. But if there aren't any natural disasters to forcibly keep you indoors and away from food, you're just going to have to set aside half a bottle of Adderall and a three-day weekend, I guess.

Eating Clean

#clean #cleaneats #eatingclean #eatclean #traindirty #organic #healthy #nourish #nutrition #fitspo #instahealth #instagood #ieatbetterthanyou #nofilter

Those of you chic girls in the technological know will immediately recognize the above #hashtags from our favorite outlet for TMI and general braggery, Instagram. In fact, there is a good chance that many of them show up on your update feed during mealtimes on the daily, accompanied by snaps of boring salads, uninspiring chicken dishes or run-of-the-mill vegetable platters. And, despite the fact that no one really cares about foodstagrams that aren't pictures of the desserts at Eleven Madison Park, girls in yoga pants will never cease to profess their love for eating clean foods via the sharing of grainy photographs of sous vide eggs and grilled asparagus.

By announcing that you "only eat clean," you can weasel your way out of being forced to try most modern day foods. Another excuse not to eat the crap that your friends ordered whilst making an appearance at obligatory birthday dinners? Yay. It also gives you multiple opportunities to preach to others as you disparagingly eye their highly processed meal choices, which is just *titillating*. I mean, everyone knows that chic girls love to judge and make others feel like shit. It just comes with the territory.

Plus, when all of your food is either raw, baked or steamed, there's no way for extra calories to be introduced during the cooking process. And if your diet revolves around only "clean" foods, there honestly isn't much that you can have. You're basically stuck with lean meat, nuts, seeds, fruits and vegetables, all of which are relatively low in fat and calories. Of course, if you're vegan or vegetarian, you get to step atop an even *higher* soapbox with an even *cleaner* body. I mean, you're basically a bird. And have you ever seen a fat bird? I don't think so.

So squawk all you want at your friend who has the audacity to open up a bag of granola in your presence. "Do you even *know* how many additives are in that?" you will shriek as your eyes widen in horror. Then take a picture of the bowl of steamed broccoli positioned strategically atop your knees, allowing your parallel thigh gap to be showcased within the square field of the image. Make sure that your can of Diet Coke and pack of Parliaments are not visible. Apply the Valencia filter, add the aforementioned hashtags, upload for your adoring followers and await hundreds of Likes. Repeat with each meal until your Instagram account looks like an ad for one of the Greenmarkets. #Instaccountability, you know?

SUPERFOODS

If there's one thing that chic girls just *adore*, it's lecturing others on things that they don't know about yet, in relation to both the fashion and dietary realms. Chic waifs are somewhat like couture hipsters who bathe on the reg, in that they love to blurt out pretentious phrases like "Oh... how have you never heard of Astaxanthin before?" and "Ohmigod, basic fish oil is *so* over. You *have* to try krill instead. I've been using it since forever!"

They discover and become *obsessed* with new superfoods and supplements every other week, abandoning ones that become too mainstream in favor of those with unpronounceable names. For example, kale, Greek yogurt and quinoa are *so* last year. Fage? Fa-who? Um, where are the mache, kefir and amaranth? And, uh, almonds and walnuts? Didn't you know that Jungle Peanuts and Sacha Inchi seeds are where it's at?

"I make my breakfast smoothies with organic collards, dandelion greens, a shot of wheatgrass, three macerated mulberries, one-fifth of a banana, the entire banana peel, noni juice, maca, bee pollen, a scoop of Green Vibrance and some maqui and acai powder," the chic girl will brag to her adoring friends when they comment on her glowing skin. "Then I add some alkaline ice cubes and chia seeds. It all tastes so amaze and keeps me satiated until dinnertime. Like, I totally forget to eat because I'm so full. You guys should really try it." It will slip her mind to mention that 1) it took her 45 minutes to choke down the brownish green goo and 2) she has three layers of Nars Albatross on her cheekbones.

She will rave about the salad that she had at lunch ("It had wakame, dulse *and* hijiki. With Chioggia beets!") or that one orgasmic vegan, gluten-free, nut-free, frisee-adorned plate from last night ("I DIE for Hen of the Woods. They're, like, my favorite type of mushroom after Matsutakes"). The only chocolate that she'll ever eat is Rawmio, since it's vegan and made with raw organic cacao nibs with a potent organic raw fungus blend and sprouted red clover. Whatever that means. But it sounds uber nutritious, so she'll take it.

The chic nutritionista's kitchen counter is cluttered with the ironic juxtaposition of bottles of both the prescription and holistic health blend varieties. I mean, when she's barely ingesting food, she has to find her nutrients somewhere, right? Her daily vitamin routine is composed of fistfuls of tablets, capsules and tinctures containing exotic fruit extracts, phytoplankton, rare earth probiotics, amino acids and all-natural stress-relief complexes. "You really have to try Wellness Formula. It's life-changing," she will chirp as she rattles the bottle of supplements excitedly. When a friend inquires about the formula's contents, she will breezily brush the comment away with an "I don't know. Antioxidants?"

It will seem as if she's speaking a foreign language with all of the cruciferous name-dropping that she commits ("Did you see Gwyneth's recipe for roasted romanesco? I think that I'll try it on the kohlrabi I got in my CSA box"). In fact, some of the supplements that she mentions will make you feel like you're sitting in on a Principles of Taxonomy course ("Oooh, let's all take shots of Moringa Oleifera!"). And, somehow, she will know more about superfood quackery than that New Age hippie who sells healing crystals and sage sticks on Christopher Street. "I feel so alive!" she will announce as she passes around her bag of camu camu-infused goji berries and tosses back shots of colloidal gold and blue-green algae.

But don't bother to try and keep up. By the time that you mention your newfound love for flax, she'll already be *over* it. Her shoulders will tense up underneath her Derek Lam top and the corners of her lips will quiver as she counters with a "Flax? Oh. Um, you should really try hemp seeds. They're, like, a lot better for you." And do not, under any circumstances, suggest any type of "fake" health food. You will lose any and all street cred that you may have once held as she narrows her eyes and spits out a seething "I don't DO muesli."

HEALTH BEVERAGES

"I'm really into Yerba Mate right now. It's like an all-natural version of coffee," the health-conscious chic girl will explain to her *très* clueless friends. "Oh, and matcha tea. They're both supposed to, like, melt fat away. Also, you *have* to try the Gingerade Kombucha. It's *amazing*. And the Green Chia one? Ob-sessed!"

What fun would there be in eating recondite superfoods if one did not have equally obscure and expensive beverages with which to wash them down? Chic girls are *all* about health brews, as can be observed in their rampant enthusiasm for juicing. But green juices aren't the only trendy vitamin-packed fluids available. And, just as with fashion, brand names are key so that people can recognize the labels and acknowledge how healthy you are.

For starters, there's GT's Kombucha, which is basically fermented tea produced from a giant mother spore. Um, ew. Thankfully, chic girls can ignore that factoid, since the wonderful company packages various flavors of the brew into chicly-labelled glass bottles that totally go with their Lululemon yoga pants. All the cool girls drink this and love to march around with them on display as they scurry around the city. Who cares if one serving is almost the same price as a takeaway lunch? And why does it matter if some of them taste like expired Snapple? You're imbibing liquid health!

Then there are Kvass, a fermented beet juice, and Kevita, a sparkling probiotic drink that tastes like salty San Pellegrino. They both come in a variety of flavors, are sweetened with stevia and have probiotics in them to keep you trim and regular. I am also a fan of Bragg's Apple Cider Vinegar drink in Ginger Spice because, like, ACV is supposedly totes good for you.

Turmeric Elixirs are also popular, but some are sweetened with fucking *honey* or *agave*, so I would proceed with caution. You really have to be very careful when approaching the beverage aisle in general. A lot of these purported "health drinks" are actually high-carb wolves in sheeps' clothing. Like, a lot of aloe drinks and brewed teas are just filled with cane sugar. How rude, right? *So* deceptive, just like my ex-friend Courtney. They're probably compulsively lying sluts who would steal your La Perla underwear, too. Ugh. Whatever. Anyway, as long as you make sure to diligently check your labels like the neurotic freak that you are, you should be fine.

If you really want to guzzle down some turmeric or aloe sans any sugar, you can look into the shots offered by a few of the juice bars. Juice Press has a bunch of them, but some of them taste terrible. One of my hippie-chic friends, Ally, gave me a Candida scare, so I went and got the totes appropriate Volcano shot from there and I almost threw up afterward. It was really not chic. So if you go that route, you should definitely add some stevia in before you pound it. Or you can always chase it with a Diet Coke. You're welcome.

Coconut Water

Everyone seems to feel the need to profess their obsession with coconut innards, be it oil, butter or milk, but this is especially so in the case of coconut water. It's like Gatorade for the chic elite. Fashionable hydration, I guess you can say? I don't know how it became like this, but coconut water consumption is endemic among the stylish population. It's literally *everywhere,* even in spite of the fair amount of sugar contained in each serving. I feel like Vita Coco is a proud sponsor of Equinox gymgoers everywhere.

But I guess that it works out in the same way as alcohol. When the chic aren't eating much, I suppose that there's some leeway in terms of carb counts that allows for coconut water binges. So, like, I guess that it's cocorexia? Whatever. All the skinny bitches are always chugging it, so it must be fine. I mean, if Miranda Kerr swears by it, then I'm *sure* that it's good for you, right?

And who can deny how amazing it is when you're hungover? It's like a salty-sweet corpse reviver. Not to mention that sipping a bottle of Zico is a great way to avoid fainting when you haven't had anything to eat all day. All of the minerals, magnesium and potassium are also conducive to rehydration when you've overdone it on the Adderall or diuretics. Your skin will look excellent, even without the help of half a bottle of Caudalie Beauty Elixir.

If you really want to maximize chicness, go for Harmless Harvest. The design is really cute in that 3.1 Phillip Lim comic book illustration kind of way from F/W12. Lime green on white with black accents? Very Proenza Schouler. Plus, the bottle is petite, so the small serving size will prevent you from binging. And it's raw!

I personally have a thing about drinking my calories, so I pour the contents of one bottle of coconut water into my giant glass Lifefactory water bottle and dilute it with an equivalent volume of Penta water. Then I refill two empty Zico bottles to get two servings for the calorie and sugar content of one. If I'm feeling really gross, I'll just refill one of those bottles with water. This way, I can still be seen carrying around and drinking from these fashionable *pièces de résistance*, even if I'm technically not ingesting any of the actual product. I just don't want to be left out, you know?

Even if you can't find your brand of choice, you can easily procure a bottle or carton of some sort from any old store in the city. Like, even the dusty, run-down bodegas hawk the stuff. Just try to stick to the unadulterated varieties because the flavored ones are teeming with sugar. And even if you can't stand the taste, just suck it up and drink some, or at least carry one around. After all, it's only the fashionable thing to do.

NON-DAIRY MILKS

Who drinks cow's milk anymore? It's just *so* Middle America. Didn't you know that vegan milks are all the rage right now? Excluding soy, of course, because it's too prosaic and apparently not very good for you. Unless, of course, you're grabbing Starbucks. Then you should *only* do soy.

When milk shopping at any health food store, you are offered a plethora of choices, such as those made from barley, oat, pea, quinoa, hemp, sunflower seed, almond, cashew, hazelnut, or coconut. Basically, it can be produced from anything that can be immersed in water and strained to produce an opaque runoff. Now, as a chic consumer, your main criteria when milk-shopping should be calorie count and sugar content. Grain and legume milks tend to contain more sugar due to the higher carb natures of the ingredients, so walk away from those. Ew, liquified carbs.

This leaves chic girls to pick between the nut, seed and coconut milk offerings on the shelves. Most stores will have unsweetened versions of almond and coconut milks available, in either plain, vanilla or chocolate flavors. Pick either type of blend according to your taste preferences, as both are low in calories with little to no carbs. I cannot stress enough the imperativeness of only buying unsweetened cartons. You can add your own stevia or

Splenda later on without risking your ketotic status. *Quelle horreur* should that happen, right?

All of the raw, vegan, organic, gluten-free, sustainable restaurants around town are making dairy-free alternatives to cheese out of nuts too. Like, how innovative. I even had a faux-cheese plate the other day and I could barely tell the difference, other than the fact that the blocks didn't smell, feel or taste like actual cheese. I told my other roommate, Lauren, to try some, but she was cleansing at the time and was only having Rooibos tea and biodynamic vegan wine. But I'm sure that other people would think that the macadamia nut cheese tastes just like a hunk of gouda. I think that I just have a really discerning palate.

Anyway, everyone's drinking vegan milks these days. Fashion models love that shit. Like, Karlie Kloss drinks almond milk, and have you *seen* her legs? And the Coconut Mylk at Organic Avenue? Swoon. It's like a fucking coconut milkshake. Or at least what I imagine a milkshake would taste like.

Bars

Want to see something cool? Walk over to any chic girl's desk. Open the second drawer to the right and be prepared to be amazed by a mini version of the meal replacement bar section of a small natural foods market contained within. When said chic girl is feeling woozy and begins to feel tiny beads of cold sweat form on her brow near the end of a long, food-deprived day, she will make an emergency choice from this strictly curated selection to serve as her lunch and/or dinner. Normally, she would forgo eating in general, but she just doesn't want to faint on her 11-block walk to happy hour, you know?

Plus, thanks to the exorbitant amount of time that she spent examining the labels for every protein bar at Whole Foods, she'll know the exact nutritional profile and list of ingredients for the dense rectangle that she is about to ingest. Speaking of which, not all bars are created equal. Like, don't even think about picking up any old Clif or Luna bar. Um, have you *seen* the carb contents? And don't trust "green" bars with pretty labels. Just because they're green, organic and full of "whole" ingredients doesn't mean that they're void of sugar. Date purée? Brown rice syrup? Ugh. Read your nutrition facts, people!

Some tried and true favorites include Gnu Bars, Quest

Protein Bars, BNRG Power Crunch Bars, NuGo Slim Bars, Fullbars, Health Warrior Chia Bars, Raw Crunch Bars, Macro Greens Antioxidant Superfood Bars and Kind Bars. You're, like, really lucky that the chic girls before you have narrowed down the options to exclude bars containing maltitol (a.k.a. flatulence factory fuel) or large amounts of sugar. So considerate.

Anyway, Gnu Bars are great because they contain less than 150 calories apiece, yet still provide 50% of your daily fiber requirement. And we all know how a chic girl loves herself a good bowel movement, right? Now, they don't taste *amazing*, but they're good enough. I mean, what do you expect from an eerily-moist mound that's made up of 14 grams of fiber and will only cost you 130 calories? Plus, there are, like, a bunch of flavors to suit whatever mood you're in. The Carrot Cake is palatable, and it contains only 1/3 of the amount of sugar in the Carrot Cake Bar from Clif. Unless you are mentally slow, it's pretty obvi which one you should pick.

Quest Bars hold a special place in the chic girl's heart because they are packed with protein and fiber, but are sweetened with stevia for minimal sugar content. Like, single digit status. Mind blowing, right? Most of the ingredients are natural too, and they're gluten-free! It's as if they were created with neurotic waifs in mind. The flavors are based on desserts like Strawberry Cheesecake and Cinnamon Rolls, and they actually taste somewhat similar. FYI, I have 74 of these stashed in my drawer at this very moment.

Power Crunch Bars also use Splenda and stevia to sweeten things up, and they provide a nice, light crunch when you're sick of gumming down mushy bars. These wafer-like protein bars don't come in too many flavors, but the Cookies & Creme and Wild Berry flavors are uber yum. NuGo Slim Bars are like overly chewy candy bars with moderate protein and fiber content. Make sure to floss afterward because that shit will get stuck all up in your tooth crevices.

Fullbars will provide you with yet another textural option because they are light and airy, like mutant Rice Krispie Treats. Sugar content is moderately high, at 12 grams, due to the fact that they contain fucking brown rice syrup, so tread carefully around these. But sometimes you just *need* that change in texture, you know? The same goes for Kind Bars—some, like the Cashew & Ginger Spice or Madagascar Vanilla flavors, contain very little sugar at 4 grams each. But make sure to study the labels diligently, because other varieties can contain as much as 16 grams! Ew.

Health Warrior Chia Bars are healthy and uber low in calories and sugar, even though they contain some of the reviled, aforementioned syrups. The same goes for Raw Crunch Bars, which contain flax and a bunch of other seeds. These two bars will provide different mouthfeels and nutritional offerings. The Macro Greens Chocolate & Cinnamon Antioxidant Superfood Bars are super nutritious because they have all of this shit thrown in, like vegetable powders and support herbs, so they make you feel good about eating them. That particular flavor is low in sugar, clocking in at 7 grams, but the two other flavors (Apple Lemon Ginger and Miracle Reds Berri Berri) contain a lot more. Again, use discretion when picking them out.

So many choices, so little time, right? Well, if you replace all of your meals with bars, then you should have no problem trying out a wide range of flavors and varieties. Plus, you would be able to keep a tightly controlled diet of highly accurate calorie and carb counts. You'd basically be, like, a weight loss robot. Ooh, you can get those sleek silver Charlotte Olympia heels as, like, part of your uniform. Totally symbolic.

ACUPUNCTURE

Unless you've been living under a rock, you probably know about how a lot of people are *super* into acupuncture and Eastern Medicine these days, especially for weight loss. Apparently, the acupuncture itself can accomplish all of these magical tasks, such as helping to reduce un-chic cravings, regulate blood sugar levels, normalize metabolism and reduce anxiety, which everyone knows is at the root of all binge eating sessions. The herbal formulations are supposed to help detoxify the blood and body, but they also provide the chic girl with yet another excuse to forgo consumption of actual food. Ooh, maybe this is a sign that you should buy one of those sick Asian-inspired Lover lace rompers to wear to your appointment.

My friend, Amanda, lost, like, half of her body weight after she did a month-long cleanse from one of the nearby clinics, which made me uber jelly. Naturally, I followed suit. The clinic that we went through utilizes multiple approaches to promote ~~weight loss~~ detoxification. First, they perform a thorough analysis on your body composition to determine how much fat and bloating you could stand to lose. The doctor will blab about pollution, immunity, phlegm (ew), qi and energy for a bit, and will stress the importance of exercise and moderation (yawn). Then, finally, on to the good part!

The dietary regimen includes a preliminary preparation period, a detox period and a final recovery period, during all of which you'll visit the clinic twice a week for abdominal stabbings. The acupuncture itself barely hurts, but it's really difficult to lie still unless you take, like, an Ativan before your appointment. Sometimes, your acupuncturist will attach electrodes to the needles, so you become kind of like a cute Frankenstein. Keep your phone handy to Instagram pictures of this mini science project to exhibit how healthy and in-the-know you are. You also have the option of undergoing "cupping", a slightly gross process in which the practitioner will stab you with a needle and proceed to place a hot cup over the region to draw out "bad blood". You'll be left with dark circular bruises, which means no open-back Mara Hoffman dresses for a while. But Gwyneth partakes, so I'm sure that it's kosher, right?

Anyway, back to the *très* important part. So, you'll be given these herbal concoctions that you drink over the course of your preparation, fasting and recovery periods. You can eat lightly during the preparation and recovery days, but I chose to subsist on the juice the entire time since I'm an overachiever. I thought that it would taste like kombucha, but I was sorely mistaken. It tastes like a cloying, rotten apple juice of some sort that makes you want to die whenever you plug your nose to choke it down. But Amanda raved about how refreshing it was, so I did too. The nutritionist gushed about how it's filled with all of these revitalizing enzymes and whatnot, but it just made me really, really sad. But I guess if svelteness was a food, that's what it would taste like—despair.

Afterward, though, I got really happy, because I ended up losing, like, 15% of my body weight. Totes worth it, right? I bought a super cute A.L.C. dress to congratulate myself. So, yea, I highly recommend trying it if you have the pain tolerance to do so. All of the chubby naysayers will be like, "Ohmigod, you're not eating *again?"* But this time, you can be like, "It's totally legit. I mean, the *doctor* uses *needles* to redirect my *qi*. My health insurance covers it, so, I mean, it's obvi a *medical* procedure." Plus, *everyone* is juice cleansing now, which definitely makes it seem a lot more mainstream and a bit less glamorous. And, if there are needles involved, it *has* to be good for your health, right?

GENERAL ORTHOREXIA

If you haven't noticed by now, many a chic girl is obsessed with achieving the pinnacle of health. Her diet is as clean as a whistle and there is nary a toxin floating around in her pristine bloodstream. And while many rude fist-shakers will yell out descriptors like "anorexic" or "deranged", I would like to politely disagree. If a chic girl's dietary habits were to be classified as anything, I guess they could be categorized as orthorexic. But, I mean, isn't orthorexia just a supposed "eating disorder" made up by bitter fat people?

Like, how can you label someone as having a mental disorder just because she doesn't drink soy milk or eat Oreos? Isn't the person who endlessly shoves Five Guys burgers into her mouth, all the while allowing her muffin top to grow exponentially, the one with the mental health issue? Skinny-shaming is just, like, really unfair bullying that's directed at svelte hard workers with venerable amounts of self-control. I mean, sure, the dedication and perseverance required to adhere to chic and strict dietary standards *can* border on extreme, but at least the cray is all for the better good. In the same vein that this section is aptly named, we're just trying to be healthy.

Anyway, let's go along with the presumption that orthorexia

is a real, novel species of disordered eating. If that's true, then there are some chic girls who have full blown cases of it. You can basically take almost every single tactic that was highlighted in this section and combine them to provide an accurate snapshot of the *au naturel* chic girl's diet. These girls take their eating habits to the next lev—I mean, they don't even smoke or drink Diet Coke. They drink organic locally-sourced green tea (steeped for precisely two minutes, natch) because it's full of antioxidants and catechins, whatever those are. They [shrewdly] avoid any processed grains, opting instead for spelt, millet and sorghum (that is, if they're doing carbs at all). Everything is organic, triple-filtered and hand-coddled to maturity. Nuts and dried fruit are terrifying, and don't even think about mentioning fucking *corn* in their presence. Anything that is white in color is absolutely out of the question. Some may even convulse in the presence of brioche.

The really stringent girl won't do any type of carbohydrate at all, ruing the days that carrots and sweet potatoes were first cultivated on this Earth. "Nightshades?!" she will hiss out, aghast at the presence of tomatoes in her escarole salad. "You know that the two main ingredients in Greek yogurt are mucus and sugar, right?" she will scoff when you pull out your 0% Fage and accompanying Splenda packet. Picking up a carton of free-range, vegetarian diet-fed, organic and locally-raised chicken eggs will illicit a disapproving shake of the head from her. When you pull out a packet of raw almonds and glance at her for approval, you will be met with an "I'm literally scared for your Omega-3 and 6 balances right now."

In layman's terms, she is just like every other chic girl except for the fact that she's a bit more uptight, a tad more judgmental and actually eager to partake in this style of eating. But who cares if she tiptoes on the border of unhinged? She's skinny as fuck, and her skin *glows* from within. So throw that raw, non-GMO, organic and unsulphured trail mix out of your windows, ladies, because there's a thing or two that you can learn from your orthorexic friend. "Eat to live, not live to eat," she will chant like a beanpole possessed. To live (and die) in sample sized Maje? Pass the watercress, please.

EXERCISE

Members of the chic elite are, after all, human and, thus, will occasionally fuck up on their diets. And though mere mortals may allow for some caloric slippage now and then, cheat days don't exist in the world of the intentionally emaciated. But fear not, chic hopefuls, as there is a way to remedy overdrawn calorie accounts—good ol' sweat and tears. And any excuse to go on a Lululemon shopping binge is a good thing, right?

Some chic girls can go a little overboard with their exercise regimens, calculating their workouts so that they burn every last calorie that they had consumed that day. This phenomenon has been coined as “exercise bulimia” by the media, which I guess it technically is. Everyone knows that bulimia, in any shape or form, isn't attractive, even if this variation doesn't make your teeth fall out. So, like, try to avoid reenacting that depressing cliché of fainting on the treadmill, please. But as long as you are just utilizing exercise to strengthen your body and burn off *extra* calories, you're golden.

As you can see, the people of Manhattan are infatuated with fitness. You can barely get past two city blocks without passing some sort of gym, fitness studio or outdoor exercise group whose members are oblivious to the urban cacophony surrounding them, being deeply engrossed in their Hiking Yoga excursion. I'm not one to strike warrior poses outdoors, which is why obscenely expensive ~~gimmicks~~ classes are my, and apparently many others', sweat-inducing drugs of choice.

With each passing day, another friend mentions some new, ridiculously-named exercise program that just launched with waiting lists to get onto the waiting lists. Everyone is all about either SoulCycle, Pure Barre, Physique 57, SLT or Core Fusion, with yoga sessions to "unwind" afterward. In terms of fat loss, SoulCycle or cardio at the gym are the ways to go, while everything else is pretty much for toning up already thin limbs and torsos.

I don't know why my friends continue to hold their birthday parties at SoulCycle, because I wouldn't want to spend my day of celebration trying to keep up with the instructor while feeling awkward as she barks out words of encouragement over some blaring Tiesto mix. Plus, it always feels like all of my classmates took one-too-many antidepressants before each session, and then I feel even more discouraged for not having the time of my life while wearing a SoulCycle tank top like everyone else.

Physique, Pure Barre and Bar Method are basically mash-ups of ballet, mat exercises and Pilates. As everyone knows, ballerinas are the epitome of chicness, so these classes are totes the way to go for low-intensity, yet excruciatingly painful, elegance. While the classes are not as intense as spinning, they do help to tone up wobbly bits and make you feel *the burn*. Core Fusion Barre errs more on the side of Pilates than barre method, and SLT is like Pilates on steroids with those crazy and intimidating reformer machines.

If one of those isn't your cup of tea, there are a bunch of other programs as well. You can be all cray and pay thousands of dollars for Tracy Anderson, or sign up for Barry's Bootcamp or something. But Barry's is scary and there are moments in which you fear that you might actually die. If you want something slightly less intense, Aerospace has a jump-roping class that will still leave you sopping wet and bedridden for days. You can always try out water aerobics, Crossfit or kickboxing, too. Just please do not sign up for a pole-dancing class, as stripping is the very antithesis of chic.

In sharp contrast to attitudes toward superfoods or fashion, it's better to just stick with the mainstream gyms and classes. I don't know why this is, but I advise that you just get an Equinox membership and breathe in the familiar scent of SoulCycle candles on the reg. Trust me, your life will be much easier due to the vast number of locations for both, and you can totally bond with others over how your glutes are aching after your intense MetCon3 session that morning.

So you went to town with a falafel plate during lunch? It's okay—it happens to the best of us. NOT. After you're done beating yourself up (which you should), pull on your adidas by Stella McCartney leggings (*so* cute, by the way) and lace up your Nike Free Runs, my friend, because you're in for a treat. In order to burn off the roughly 700 totes unnecessary calories that you chose to foolishly indulge in, you can either partake in one spinning sesh or endure an hour on the Stairmaster. That was fun, wasn't it? In the words of my sagely SoulCycle instructor—"I will leave this class and make better choices today." Um, yea. Yea, you will.

Um, It's Not a Fad... It's a Lifestyle

Vegetarianism

"It's just *really* sad. I watched a movie on Netflix about it," the doe-eyed waif will whimper as she wraps her fave Margiela Mongolian goat hair shrug tightly around her thin frame while hoisting the chain strap of her Ohmigod-touch-this-it's-*sooo*-soft lambskin Reissue 2.55 onto her shoulder. "That's why I don't eat meat."

One quick glance through a chic girl's closet will reveal her penchant for ostentatious furs and general lack of regard for animals' well-beings in the name of fashion. So why the abstemious vegetarian diet? To automatically disqualify 75% of the most lardaceous dishes on restaurant menus, duh.

In the same way that crying gluten sensitivity allows the chic girl to abstain from partaking in the joy that simple carbohydrates provide, chirping about her vegetarian lifestyle will save her from having to eat from passing plates of salt-ridden charcuterie or sauce-asphyxiated morsels of saturated fat at dinner parties or events. Um, do you know how many calories can be averted by *combining* these two ~~lies~~ tactics? *Bajillions*.

"Ohmigod, I can't eat *anything*!" she will whine and pout, as if she weren't actually beaming inside. By effectively eliminating most items from the Standard American Diet from her "allowed foods" list, said chic girl can comfortably reject all food that is offered to her without drawing concern for her mental health. She just has a really delicate stomach and respectable morals, you know?

In reality, bitch could care less about bunnies and cows, unless they were used to make her Acne angora sweater or Helmut Lang leather jacket, like, really soft. Truth be told, the only animal whose company she actually enjoys is her teacup Yorkie named Paris or Chloé. And that’s only *some* of the time.

But if faux-swooning over Youtube videos of pygmy goats or signing petitions for feral kittens outside of Whole Foods will allow her to evade Kobe meatballs or duck fat fries without raising suspicion, then so be it. You know that street meat goes straight to your thigh gap, right? Eew.

Oh, why not veganism? Um, that doesn’t really work because then, like, cheese wouldn’t be allowed. And how do you expect a girl to make it through her low carb purgatory without the occasional piece of Sottocenere? That’s just cruel.

The Baby Food Diet

Take a good look at Abbey Lee Kershaw and Hedi Slimane. See their jutting cheekbones and bulging eyeballs? Yours can *totally* be like that too, so long as you're willing to adhere to the uber cutesy diet that these two effortlessly chic Skeletors have been known to follow.

Now, everyone knows that digestion isn't very glamorous. The act of mastication is, in itself, so very vulgar, and then that nasty bolus of calorific horror settles into your distended stomach, stirring up a whirlwind of gas and discomfort as it waits for *hours* to be broken down. After that harrowing process, a trillion fat globules get sent directly to your upper arms and inner thighs. And then, well, you know…something *really* un-chic happens in *le toilette*.

But what if you could bypass all of that unpleasantry and just follow a really adorable diet that consists of only a few hundred calories a day? And, like, your stomach will stay flat since it's not filled with festering kale and noxious fumes. Ohmigod, tell me more, right? Enter: the Baby Food Diet.

You don't have to chew anything since the blender did that for you. Portion control won't be an issue either since all of the stores carry single-servings with really low calorie counts. And, like,

I guess that babies need clean and well-rounded food or something because, like, all of the ingredients are things that you've heard of before and are actually good for you. It's like a juice fast, but with a little more substance and a little less lawnmower drippings. But, like, *waaay* more affordable, so you can use all of the money that you save on some unflavored Pedialyte, which is really just like a zero-calorie coconut water.

Plus, thanks to all of the crazy and demanding yoga mommies decked out in Lululemon with their obscenely expensive strollers, Whole Foods has really upped their game in the baby food aisle. There's seriously a flavor for whatever type of mood that you might be in, so don't even worry about lack of variety. It's like chic girl heaven. Make sure you get there early though, so you won't have to fight with the colicky toddler in the Missoni Bugaboo over the last "zucchini banana & amaranth".

Ella's Kitchen and Plum Organics are good for your basic blends of fruits and vegetables, but I swear that the marketing team at Earth's Best was targeting chic/orthorexic adults when naming their product lines. "Antioxidant Blends"? "Super Fruits"? "Gourmet Meals and Seasonal Harvest"?! Um, yea, okay. Like 6-month olds care about that kind of shit.

So, apparently, Tracy Anderson (bless her heart) suggests that one should consume 14 jars per day. Um, no. It's not like we're headed into famine or something. A couple of jars or pouches should suffice and, even then, you should be watching your carb intake. That means NO all-fruit blends, you fat fuck. Make sure to pick vegetable-heavy varieties, though those can be sugarific also. I mean, even "spinach + apples + rutabagas" has 8 grams of carbs after adjusting for fiber. Ugh. Who knew that babies were such sugar whores? It’s just, like, really unfair for all of the other customers who are trying to watch their figures.

The Air Diet

Every wannabe Carrie Bradshaw (or Charlotte York if you're *really* annoying) yearns to achieve maximal chicness with minimal effort. And nobody can do posh like the French, right? Even their *diets* ooze superior elegance that we ugly Americans could only aspire to attain.

Like, take the Air Diet, or *L'Air Fooding* as French *Grazia* dubbed it. God, even the name is so chic, I DIE. So anyway, you basically pretend to eat whatever the hell you want, without actually allowing it touch your lips. Naysayers and physicians will be like, "Ohmigod, that's called anorexia!", but, um, no. Anorexia is what my roommate, Sydney, has, and she won't even go near food without having a twitching episode. This is, like, a lot healthier psychologically.

I mean, I totally get it. Everyone knows that enjoying food is an experience, and this diet allows you to immerse yourself in the whole process until the actual eating part. But you still get to order your meal, pay for it, cut it up, smell the aromas and Instagram pictures of your drool-worthy plate. You just don't absorb all of the calories and fat associated with ingesting the actual food. It's like you're a chic French diet mime who traded eating for the right to talk. Ooh, maybe you can buy a really cute A.P.C. striped shirt to go with your performance. So authentic.

It's not like you don't eat at all, either. You still get to binge on all of the *la soupe à l'eau* (translation: chic soup with an uber pretentious name) that you want. Oh, you want to know what's in it? Um, I had the recipe right here. Hold on. Oh, here it is. Boiled water and sea salt. Hm. But sea salt has, like, a lot of minerals in it, right? How nutritious.

So, yea. It seems like the majority of my friends have been on this diet for a really long time. Like even before that issue came out. What trendsetters. I mean, it's a great way for cutting calories, you know? As a bonus, it's not even restrictive! Like, you can help yourself to all of the fancily named soup and air that you want. And, like, a variety of air at that. Just stroll through the perfume section at Barney's or traipse through Le Labo when you're feeling bored with the plain, bourgeoisie oxygen around you. And if you're feeling especially ravenous (um, binge eating disorder, anyone?) you can practice some yoga breathing. It's like dietary meditation. Kay, now Ocean Breath, everyone.

The Paleo Diet

While cavemen might not have been very fashion-forward, they apparently knew how to be skinny motherfuckers. The Museum of Natural History really needs to slim down the mannequins in the exhibit to reflect this, don't you think? So inaccurate. Anyway, this hunter-gatherer-centric diet is very simple in that it has one rule—only eat shit that Betty Flinstone would have prepared.

For those of you who are unfamiliar with history, this means that Kettle Chips and peanut butter are no-goes. Anything processed, such as Lean Cuisines, or foods that require relatively modern technology to produce, such as grains, are not allowed. Neither are dairy products, refined sugars, legumes, potatoes, processed oils or alcohol. Yup, even alcohol. No, they did not have "Stone Age" vodka or sugar-free "Bedrock" Red Bull back then. Yes, I am positive.

Anyway, you're basically allowed to have wild seafood, organic eggs, grass-fed game, vegetables, fruits and some nuts. The idea behind this style of eating is that humans, as a species, have not evolved much since the era of our cave-dwelling ancestors. That is, our digestive systems are largely genetically similar to those of dinosaurs and aren't fully adapted to the vast changes in diet that have occurred since the dawn of the agricultural age. Like, we're not that great at digesting the majority of the shit foods that line supermarket shelves today. Yes, even the shelves at Whole Foods.

By following a paleolithic diet, however, we would be providing our bodies with ideal foods to which our digestive systems are genetically adapted. When we are better able to process and absorb nutrients from these easily digested foods, we would be more capable of achieving optimal health.

But who really cares about primal strength and surly shit like that? Not any of my friends, despite the fact that everyone I know has "gone Paleo". What we love about this diet is the amount of control and restriction that it provides the user. You can basically reject most foods so long as you can come up with some inane reason as to why. "I'm only channeling cavewomen who lived in the Northern Hemisphere, and I don't think *those* were native to that region," you can say with a dismissive sniff as you swat away a platter of seasonal stone fruit. Um, apricots have a lot of carbs, didn't you know?

Plus, the diet itself is just really trendy. It's like the new Dukan Diet, which was originally the new Atkins, which was basically the new Cabbage Soup Diet. You'll probably be consuming the same meals that you normally ate, but can now affix the hip label of "Paleo" to your dietary habits. But don't do that shit where you put goat's milk butter in your coffee or inhale bushels of avocados in one sitting—no-carb calories *are* still calories, after all.

THE RIDICULOUSLY LOW CARB DIET

In the world of the chic, all of the inhabitants are consumed with keeping their carb intakes as close to zero as humanly possible. Throw any generic food product at a chic girl and she can spit back its estimated carbohydrate content in mere seconds. And, as if she were a neurologist treating childhood epilepsy, she knows the ins and outs of the ketogenic diet like the back of her Rodin Crema-slathered hand.

Though she may have no idea what mitosis is, or how photosynthesis works, any legitimate chic girl could pass a PhD-level Nutrition exam with flying colors. "In order to get into a state of ketosis, you need to deplete the glycogen stores in your liver and muscles before even tapping into your fat energy sources. To do that, you have to keep your net carbohydrate intake below 25 grams a day," she will prattle off expertly, though she may not even have the faintest idea what she is actually talking about.

Basically, she knows that the lower your carbohydrate intake, the more fat you will end up burning. Thus, being the borderline-psychotic overachiever that she is, she will set an upper limit of approximately 5 grams of net carbohydrates per day for herself.

Plus, carbs are totes unnecessary. No one has ever looked

cute while gorging on a slice of pizza or inhaling a burrito. But nibbling on a piece of asparagus or noshing on a sliver of Pecorino is just adorbs. They're like low glycemic *pièces de résistance* that compliment your Zac Posen cocktail dress. Bread used to be the official food of peasants, just so you know.

"I only eat foods that are green or white," were the first words that my soon-to-be-future roommate, Lauren, ever muttered to me. No mention of her name, age or hometown—nothing. That's how seriously a true chic girl take her carbohydrate consumption—it defines who she is.

"What do you mean?" I had asked innocently like a clueless martian. Mind you, I still wore leggings and thought Greek Yogurt parfaits were healthy at the time. (I know, I know—don't judge me.)

Lauren, bless her heart, had then taken me under her wing, expertly guiding me into my current status of perpetual ketosis. We basically subsist on kale, spinach, avocados, egg whites, cheese, white fish and chicken breasts. And what can I say? I'm obsessed. The fat just melted off like butter (which is *totally* allowed, by the way). Like, I never want to belong to any other metabolic state of mind. It's just so simple, and *everyone's* doing it. I mean, just saunter into a Fashion Week after-party and it'll reek of Chanel Chance and ketones. *So* chic.

So you can go the high fat route à la Atkins, or limit your fat consumption in the way of Dukan practitioners. Either way, you'll lose the flab and be super taut. But you can never go wrong with the Green and White Diet, the secret weapon of fashionistas in the know. And, while trends may come and go, there is one combination that will always be in style—ketosis breath and look of death. #Chic

The Strategic Starvation Diet

"You just don't eat for, like, 18 hours a day," the chic girl will explain when concerned friends inquire about her new stringent diet *du jour*. "But you totally get to have balanced meals for the other 6! It was on *the news*. They tested it on mice and they, like, totally lived longer. Ew."

Intermittent fasting is like a godsend for the chic. Apparently, it's actually really healthy and has a bunch of scientific studies published to back it up. Not that the chic girl will ever read them, of course. But if positive results actually exist, then there's actually something to validate her cray!

I mean, what kind of diet condones extended periods of starvation? It's as if this way of eating was made up specifically with chic bitches in mind. Not to mention that it's supposedly uber effective! Like, in clinical trials, researchers found that overweight participants who utilized intermittent fasting lost way more fat than those who ate the *same* meals spread throughout the day. I *knew* that whole "6 mini meals a day" adage was total bullshit!

Of course, the chic girl is just an extreme case of human, so she'll narrow her eating window to 2 hours or so. Some deranged bitches may even aim for 20 minutes! Talk about efficiency.

There's an even wackier version of this method that's been named the "Bulletproof Diet", whatever that means. Basically, you drink black coffee with butter or coconut oil stirred in so that you don't get hungry while in your fasted state. Um, that sounds like a lot of unnecessary calories. And chic girls don't get plagued with hunger—we like to refer to it as "getting off track". Like, seriously? Drinking butter? That's not even *real* fasting. People have no willpower nowadays.

Supporters of this way of eating suggest that people snack on healthy foods during their feeding periods, like bananas and apples. Um, bananas are *super* starchy. And apples? Did you know that apples don't actually have much nutritional value? The only real benefit that comes from apples is from pectin, which will help to regulate digestion. But since chic girls already consume astronomical amounts of fiber, they won't be receiving many benefits from munching on apples. They can totally get their Vitamin C from elsewhere. Ohmigod, you're learning, like, so much from me. This might as well be a textbook!

I suggest that you nibble on a piece of cheese or veggies during your allotted eating time. That way, you can totally maximize ketosis and burn as much fat as fucking possible. I mean, Emily Blunt's character in *The Devil Wears Prada* totally knew what she was doing. She was just *way* ahead of her time. Like, don't you want to be one stomach flu away from sample size too?

The Raw Food Diet

This one's for the extremists, of which there are many in the upper echelons of the chic. Basically, you stick to a diet of uncooked veggies all day long, with the occasional piece of fruit thrown in. As expected, these bitches are skinny as fuck and look *great* in just about anything. They also absorb, like, maximal nutrients and have beautiful skin and hair. Plus, they get to lecture and judge others all day long about the importance of enzymes and whatnot. These skinny twigs can also consume bushels of allowed foods and still keep their daily calorie counts in the hundreds. Totes ideal, if you can stomach it, I mean. But have you ever *tried* raw broccoli or mushrooms? Ew.

If you've lost all sensory input from your tastebuds, as can happen when on frightening amounts of amphetamines, this is the perfect lifestyle for you. You can be like a super svelte panda bear and nosh on stalks of celery or fistfuls of curly kale all day. You'll lose heaps of weight and will have a spotless digestive tract, I'm sure. Just be proactive about taking, like, 15 Beano with each meal. Gas isn't cute, even if it's being caused by adorable produce like grape tomatoes and baby carrots.

Some people will get all technical and allow themselves to have sashimi, but staunch raw foodists will shake their heads at this practice. I don't see what's wrong with it, especially since sushi is, like, so yum. Anyway, soaked nuts and sprouted seeds are allowed, but make sure to watch how much you eat. They're still packed with calories and, thus, aren't totally conducive to rapid fat obliteration.

People on the raw food diet love to chirp about mental clarity and feelings of euphoria, but I think that they're just really happy because they can slip into Gareth Pugh leather leggings without putting up a struggle. I highly doubt that weeping into bowls of raw radicchio and consuming bland vegetables dressed in the salt of my tears would make me feel vibrant and more alive. I mean, I would be completely ecstatic about sticking to a strict diet of copper pennies and shards of glass if it, too, left me with a 3-inch thigh gap. But to each her own, I suppose.

It's also well known that a lot of working models are technically raw foodies since they basically just consume cauliflower smoothies and piles of wilted spinach. No wonder they always look so sad. But have you seen their hip bones? Um, yea.

So I totally just ordered a raw organic vegan Kale Dulse Salad and a cold-pressed coffee from Seamless. They better fucking hurry before all of the nutrients break down. Ooh, do you think calories can break down over time too? Let's hope so. Enzymes, here I come!

The One Food Diet

Basically, anyone who lacks even a smidgen of self-control should consider this dietary tactic. It allows no leeway for excuses or exceptions so long as you follow just one simple rule: consume only one type of food.

When you define vague dietary rules, such as allowing low-carb or liquid items, you'll find that the hungry fatass within will convince herself that certain foods fit the guidelines. I mean, butterscotch pot de creme is technically liquid, right? And an entire stick of butter covered in guacamole is totes low-carb. Inhaling, like, three bowls of blood orange sorbet doesn't constitute cheating on a raw food diet, either...

Stop. Just stop. You obvi have issues with following rules, oh voracious one. Technicalities are just fancy excuses for the dietarily inept, and one shouldn't be allowed to make risky, body composition-altering decisions when starving and delirious. So do as the OCD-inflicted waifs do and pick one food with which to thoroughly familiarize yourself to the point of disgust for the next two weeks.

You won't have to waste time obsessing over meal planning or calculating nutritional contents. It's basically like putting your diet on auto-pilot as you graze on your one allowed food in a fat-shedding haze. Honestly, you can pick whatever you want, since you'll likely get sick of it and gradually begin to eat less and less as time goes on. Like, did you know that Uma Thurman once went on an ice cream diet? She lost 25 pounds over a six-week period. On ice cream. ON ICE CREAM.

Now, I don't suggest that you pick the congealed, sweetened mucus of dairy cows as your food of choice, as that's just, like, not really a good starting point. Pick something like tomatoes, or green apples, or avocados. Bananas and grapes work also, but do keep in mind that they are quite high in sugar. My personal choices are either eggs or grapefruit with Splenda. Whatever you choose, make sure to stick with it. That's all there is to it.

Some proponents believe that partaking in the consumption of only one type of food allows your body to become more efficient at digesting and metabolizing it, but I'm not sure. I mean, I guess it makes sense. But who really gives a fuck about all of that health-boosting mumbo jumbo? The real reason that this diet is so attractive and effective is because it helps to teach you a lesson in discipline and restraint. By sticking to this diet for just a short while, you'll see that you're more than capable of controlling yourself when it comes to impulsive food-related decisions.

It's like dietary therapy, but without having to visit an overpriced psychiatrist who just nods along and asks you obvious questions about how you *feel* about that time you ate a lobster roll. Um, I feel like shit, okay? You didn't need to remind me. That's why I'm only allowing myself zucchini slices for the next month, duh.

The Two Cup Diet

Did you know that your stomach is only the size of your fist? So why are you stuffing it until you can't breathe? Um, I don't care if you're a firm believer in Volumetrics—that method only works if you're feasting on organic iceberg lettuce and sparkling water.

Now, getting bariatric surgery done costs roughly $30,000. Trust me, I went to go get an estimate. The doctor was actually really rude and scoffed at me during the consultation, which I really took offense to. He was all, "Um, you know that this is for, like, clinically obese people, right?" So I was like, "Er, yea. It's called preventative medicine, natch." And then he, like, *totally* rolled his eyes at me and said in a condescending tone, "You obvi don't qualify for the procedure, especially since your BMI totes falls into the underweight category. Sorrz." I'm not an expert in medical law or anything, but I think that's called discrimination. Horrible bedside manner, not to mention illegal, no? I really need to call my dad's attorney about this.

Anyway, my friend, Melissa, found a totally cheap alternative to getting your stomach stapled until it's the size of a walnut. She learned it from a group of 14-year old Latvian models that she shared a room with during Milan Fashion Week. You basically take two tiny Dixie cups and fill them with whatever food you might please, though preferably of the low-calorie, low-carb and low-fat variety. Then you can enjoy your mini feast without worrying about portion control. It takes the stomach roughly four hours to empty, so you can set an alarm on your iPhone for four hour intervals to remind you of when you're allowed to have another two cups. Um, genius, right? And who said that teenaged models needed to stay in school to have good heads on their shoulders?

Don't abuse this system by using the red plastic cups of beer pong infamy, though. You're not an obese retired frat boy living it up in Murray Hill. By Dixie cups, I'm referring to the uber cutesy 3 oz. waxed paper ones that are meant for gargling in the bathroom. If you want to take it to the next lev, you can also use tiny utensils, like oyster forks, to slow down your consumption and increase satiety. There was this one girl that I interned with who carried around a tiny Tiffany & Co. silver baby spoon with her everywhere. Totally crazy, yet *totally* chic. Did I mention that she weighed, like, 85 pounds?

So who cares if you look like an unhinged betch for scarfing down tiny bites of wild mushroom fricassee from a mouthwash-delivery vessel using a toddler's fork? You'll be laughing all the way past the antiseptic-scented waiting room of a really rude weight loss surgeon's shabbily decorated Upper East Side clinic while your critics slowly begin to qualify for Lap-Band installation. Um, who said that preventative medicine had to cost a year's worth of college tuition? People with no self-control, obvi.

The HCG Diet

Only a batshit cray person would willingly stab herself repeatedly while wincing and bellowing in pain, right? Um, yes, but that mentally unstable waif wielding the 25 gauge needle sure is tiny. Enter the HCG Diet, a regimen in which one is required to inject oneself with a variety of vitamins and hormones while subsisting on a maximum of 500 calories per day. HCG, or Human Chorionic Gonadotropin, is basically a hormone produced by pregnant women soon after conception for... I don't know. The guy who came up with this shit said that it suppresses your appetite and helps with fat loss, or whatever. Anyway, its use as a weight loss agent is, like, really frowned upon by the FDA, which *everyone* knows must mean that it *totally* works. Like, remember ephedra? And phentermine? Uh, yea.

It's really easy. You basically follow an ultra low-calorie, low-carbohydrate, low-fat, high-protein diet (uh, don't we regardless?) and give yourself daily injections of Vitamin B-12 and HCG in your hips and thighs, respectively. A physician or medical professional has to hand them over, so expect to pay a pretty penny (or 60 thousand) for a three-week program. If you're feeling super ambitious, you can also drag the whole thing out for six weeks!

Everyone will be like, "Er, of course you're losing weight. You're only eating 500 calories each day!" Ohmigod, really? Thanks for the news flash. I totally didn't know that. Um, of course anyone will lose weight on a 500-calorie diet, you observant twats. But who (other than an anorexic ballerina) actually has the discipline to stick to those numbers? Uh, a really chic girl who just blew one week's pay on dietary heroin, that's who.

So even if HCG isn't actually clinically proven to assist with fat loss or appetite suppression, who really cares? Even if you had spent hundreds of dollars on sterile syringes filled with Flinstones vitamins diluted in Diet Sprite, you would still have an obligation to stick to the accompanying regimen. It's called financial responsibility, people!

But, oh Chic One, how come we can't just use the homeopathic drops that they sell on Amazon? I don't want to hurt myself, you say. I really don't like needles, you cry out. Um, in case you haven't been paying attention, there's a concept called “No Pain, A Lotta Gain”. And it's just, like, really literal in this case. Don't you know that any and all injectables are, like, totes legit? I mean, just because you rub the botulism toxin all over your skin doesn't mean that you're going to do shit about your crow's feet or laugh lines. You're just going to have a really dirty face. But inject some Botox all up in those crevices? Um, hello Bruce Jenner!

Besides, didn't you know that “homeopathic” is just Latin for “faker than a Canal Street Murakami Multicolore Monogram Speedy 25”? Ew.

The Cabbage Soup Diet

"I lost, like, 10 pounds in 3 days," the chic girl will announce with widened eyes to all of her entranced comrades. "I didn't even know that I had that much to lose!"

Going on the cabbage soup diet is akin to complaining about having to fly home for the holidays or binge drinking over Memorial Day Weekend—it's just ingrained in American culture. Eating disordered betches of yore have passed this timeless diet on from generation to generation and, as unglamorous as it may be, it still prevails as a magic bullet of sorts to this day. So when you need to get skinny stat, show a little patriotic spirit and boil up a giant vat of cabbage and under-seasoned water. Your tummy won't thank you, but your thigh gap sure will.

You can binge if you'd like, but I'm sure you won't want to. The soup isn't particularly enthralling to the taste buds, but the parboiled vegetables will help to satisfy the vacuous pit that is your empty stomach. And, even if you stuff yourself senseless with the tasteless broth, you'll still probably only consume a couple of hundred calories a day. Just don't try to stand up too quickly, or you might just faint from chic overload!

Some variations of the diet allow other foods, such as

bananas and meat, but you really shouldn't try to stray from tradition. Like, what would your ancestors say? They would likely shake their pin curls in disappointment.

The basic recipe calls for cabbage (duh), celery, mushrooms, tomatoes, peppers, onions, carrots, pre-made bouillon cubes and your seasonings of choice. Sounds super yum, right? Um, this is when you're supposed to nod and be like, "Ohmigod, delish."

Anyway, I wouldn't bother adding onions or carrots since they're uber starchy. I just don't want to get kicked out of ketosis, you know? Come to think of it, throw those tomatoes out too. That bouillon just seems totes unnecessary also. Okay, so our soup will basically consist of mineral water and cabbage, I suppose. But now we're, like, totally doing the One Food Diet too. And Paleo! And, like, this is uber vegan-friendly. Gawd, talk about multi-tasking.

The I-Can't-See-It Diet

If you're a fixture on the fashion industry's party circuit, you are well aware of the *au courant* set's penchant for microscopic portions of disgustingly decadent food. I mean, what exactly is the purpose of serving miniature cupcakes? Is this a test? Like, what's with the tiny sandwiches and cheeseburgers? Is the bread just there to keep your fingers clean? And someone *please* explain to me the obsession with canapès and fried puffs. All I see are fat and carbs sharing real estate on a tray smothered in grease and shame. It's actually really confusing yet insulting yet intriguing yet tempting yet cute yet revolting, all at the same time.

Am I supposed to eat it? I think I am. I mean, these kind caterers have already done all of the hard work and cut everything into tiny, guilt-free smidgens. And how terrible could everything be when the portion sizes are so adorable? That grilled truffle oil-infused gruyere sandwich can't be *so* bad for me, right? It's only, like, half the size of my Amex card. And that microscopic scone? It's the size of a quarter! Having one doesn't make me irresponsible!

Wait a minute. Ohmigod, are people watching? Do I look poor? How come no one else is eating? Should I stop? I think I just saw that blogger pop a tiny piece of fried macaroni and cheese into his mouth. Or did he? I repeat, is this a test?

There is a reason that all of the offerings at such glamorous parties are bite-sized enigmas of congealed cheese and bacon grease. They're your cheat treats! Enjoying a few tiny morsels of forbidden food is totes acceptable, so long as you don't carry around a plate laden with them. As a reward for all of the other 364 days a year that you deny yourself of such scrumptious evils, you are allowed this one window of glorious opportunity to indulge in two or, daresay, three pieces of wanton abandon.

Oh, but the fashion crowd is a clever one. While each itty-bitty hors d'oeuvre might *seem* relatively innocuous, it is still a miniature recreation of something that you would never be caught dead eating in front of Anna Wintour. Thus, you must wolf it down as surreptitiously as possible while still keeping your composure. And in that is where the genius lies.

After committing such a deplorable act as inhaling a mini brownie in three seconds flat while crouched down behind a crowd of fashion photographers, you are overcome with remorse and shame. What has become of you? Have you no self control? It wasn't even worth it! That's it—no more food for the rest of the night! You will then ration out a mini green juice for the rest of the evening in hopes that it will at least help to dilute your transgressions.

Do you see what just happened? You got your junk food fix, yet your calorie count for the day will be kept low by the guilt that overwhelms you. If you're lucky, the remorse will spill over into the next day. Maybe even the rest of the week! Do you know what just happened? It's called psychology.

THE I'M-FUCKING-RICH-AND-GLAMOROUS DIET

For the impossibly chic girl, it's raining oysters, sashimi and tartare every night, with a guarantee of accompanying champagne showers. She loves to order seafood towers for the table and is *obsessed* with rhubarb mignonette. "I'm basically on a raw food diet, you know," she will explain to her friends as she persuades them into doing a $300 caviar tasting. "Just a really fancy one."

Or is black & blue filet mignon considered raw? Whatever. The chic girl loves her steak, especially if it's of the Kobe Wagyu variety. She'll do lobster or butterfish or even sea bream, but forgoes salmon because it's "*so* 2011". "I only do lox when I have Eggs Norwegian at Balthazar," she will say with a sniff as she peruses limited menus with disdain. "And I'm talking about *Paris* Balthazar, *not* the one on Spring."

She is like a culinary hipster in the sense that she basically shuns anything that would be available to the general public at Food Emporium. Um, farro risotto? With fucking *kale*? You better back away slowly before she scratches your face in frustration. How *dare* you offer her that. She doesn't *do* proletarian foods, didn't you know?

Basically, she will turn up her perfectly rhinoplasty job at the foods of mere mortals, rolling her eyes if someone suggests going out for pizza and snarling in disgust at the mention of gourmet burgers. "I tried a cheeseburger for the first time whilst on holiday in London last year," she will say as she lets out a harrowing sigh. "It was the worst experience of my entire life."

"Cava is *not* champagne!" she will vehemently cry out, snatching the menu away from the basic bitch who had the audacity to suggest it in her presence. "And oysters from *New Jersey*? Get the fuck out of my face."

This emaciated diva loves herself a good tasting menu, even *if* it consists of, like, 18 courses. But haven't you noticed how all of the nicer restaurants, like Per Se and Daniel, are basically just never-ending parades of microscopic low-carb morsels? Obvi the people in the kitchen get the picture! And as for dessert, this lavish betch never partakes—she's just *so* full, you know?

So be it foie grais brûlée, organic rabbit rillettes or diver scallop carpaccio, this extravagant girl knows how to execute the zero-carb diet in style. And while other chic ladies around town may have to sacrifice pricey food in favor of fashion, this is never an issue for this rich bitch (or, perhaps, her sugar daddy). For the girl on the FRaG Diet, compromise is never an option.

Hide It, Betch

Black

You can't really make it one city block without seeing some chick decked out in black on black on black. *Très chic, non*? No. There's a reason for this, and it's not because she was trying to coordinate her outfit with the color of her soul. Bitch was having a fat day, but she doth hath approached the heinously unattractive problem with finesse.

Everyone knows that the color black has magical slimming properties—I guess you could call it monochromatic sorcery. It can disguise bloating, swelling, food stains and general disarray. Chic girls exploit this by shrouding themselves in somber getups to hide the fact that they lost all self-control and indulged in those three Wheat Thins the night before. Though, to the general public, these displays of darkness may seem uber fashionable and mysterious in that Rick Owens kind of way, those in the know will recognize it as a sartorial walk of shame of sorts. The girl who had no self-control.

Now, if a really skinny girl wears an all-black ensemble, she's just being an asshole and/or is Taylor Momsen. We get it, we get it. Ooh, you look sooo skinny. You exude restraint and ketones, you ano bitch. Now, take off the leather leggings and go put on a Mary Katrantzou dress because YOU CAN, you figurative cow. Leave the black for us whales.

But I digress. Black is totes amaze when you're feeling like an overflowing mound of shit. Bonus points if you can find oversized black sunglasses to take over half of your face, in the styles of the sisters Olsen. That way, no one can see the shame and manic depression that cloud your face when you lock eyes with the equally evil twin brother of the Kouign Amann that you had inhaled just a few hours prior.

Oversized swing or fur coats add a layer of chicness that won't cling to your flab-tabulous upper arms. And, be it leggings, stockings, pants or a maxi skirt, be sure to cover up your cream-and-sugar-taking cankles. They swell when you eat, didn't you know?

Spanx

In the bleakest of times, the tightest of undergarments are required. Buried deep within every chic girl's closet lies a pair of Spanx or some other type of control top underwear. Perhaps they are camouflaged in the very back of her drawer of workout gear, or shoved into one of the pockets of her iconic Max Mara winter coat. Though she will keep it well hidden for fear of her friends rummaging through her dresser, she will be well aware of its exact coordinates at all times should bloating decide to pay a visit.

"Ohmigod, these *aren't* Spanx," she will hiss out in protest when caught lycra-handed. "They're seamless underwear. I *totally* forgot that I even have these. I just bought them, like, a really long time ago for when I wear my Herve Leger dress. You know how I abhor panty lines! And commando is *so* not chic."

Very convincing, but everyone knows that the chic can smell fear from a mile away. "Ohmigod, you have Spanx?" her rude friend, who is probably named Courtney, will say with a disbelieving scoff. "I thought only *plus-sized* girls wear those," she will add with a sniff, all the while making a mental note to burn her own pair upon arriving at home for fear that she might be met with the same judgmental eyes.

Spanx are like your embarrassing childhood friend whose existence you try to keep hidden from everyone, despite the fact that you absolutely adore her. She understands all of your flaws and tries her best to make everything better, which you really, really appreciate. But the fact is that you'd rather have everyone else think that you're perfect in that you don't actually *have* the aforementioned flaws. But the mere mention of Spanx's name will unravel all of your hard work and unrelenting efforts in tricking the world. Plus, she has a really big mouth and no sense of social decency. What if she divulges all of your adipose secrets? Now, we can't be having any of that.

So while you may just worship your Spanx for nipping and tucking in all of the right places, you must learn to keep your love affair a secret. You just don't want to be *that* girl who wears spandex *anything*, you know?

Boho Chic

"I'm really into maxi skirts right now," the bloated chic girl will say as she sucks in her tummy. "Mary Kate is my spirit animal. I also read in *Elle* that peasant blouses and kimono jackets are *totally* making a comeback."

We all know that Nicole Richie, Sienna Miller, the twins Olsen and Kate Moss have reached the pinnacle of chicness with their disheveled displays of utter perfection. Isabel Marant is the truth, Maiyet is perf, and Anna Sui makes us swoon like no other. But chic girls don't just love boho looks for the effortlessly cool vibes that they give off. Let's be truthful here—they hide our lady lumps.

Not only are flowy chiffon shirts and gauzy embroidered dresses super adorbs, they're also great for hiding the occasional belly bulge or chafing thighs situation that may arise due to uncontrolled binges on peanut butter M&Ms. Plus, they drape beautifully, which everyone knows is uber important to the chic girl on fat days. "I *love* my Band of Outsiders maxi dress," she will chirp with manic eyes. "It just hangs *so* well."

The forgiving cuts mean that your flabby upper arms and blubbery calves won't be asphyxiated by clothes that used to fit. I mean, you're already aware that you've become a total heifer—you don't need to be constantly reminded, right? Like, I don't understand those girls who still don their too-tight silk Theory shirts when they've obvi outgrown them. Why would you want to highlight your complete and utter lack of discipline?

Bohemian clothes also work for the emaciated, because the way that they hang off of your bones is just *divine*. You really can't go wrong with this type of look. Plus, when going boho chic, you can layer on as much crap as you want! The more layers, the better. No one will even question you as to why you're dressed as a Tompkins Square Park bag lady. They'll be like, "Ohmigod, where'd you get that ratty cardigan? Carven? Rick Owens? *So* cute."

So when you're feeling like a PSA for obesity, don't wallow in self-hatred and loathing. Embrace the opportunity to have some fun! Pull on your Tibi maxi skirt, your Chloe boots and a vintage poncho of some sort. And while everyone is ooh-ing and aah-ing over your breezy ensemble, you can ruminate on your past and future dietary choices. I mean, just because boho works to conceal your weight gain doesn't mean that you've been given freedom to graze on Compost Cookies. Because there *is* such a thing as boho overload. Her name is Vanessa Hudgens.

One Size Down

If you really want to fuck with your sanity, you can go with this tactic. Basically, you only buy clothing that would fit a skinnier version of your current self. That way, you *have* to lose weight. I mean, it's just really irresponsible to pay $300 for that sleeveless Kenzo dress and never wear it, right? Yes, even if it *was* on sale.

I know plenty of cray betches who employ this method of mind-fuckery. There's one that stares back at me from the mirror every morning! By only buying clothes that are one size too small, you're basically forcing yourself to lose weight. It's also really unfair to the clothing if you don't. They just want to be worn! Why should they have to suffer just because you opted for a malted Black & White milkshake instead of an extra dry cappuccino? *So* not worth it, by the way.

Every girl dreads those days when she has somewhere uber important to go to, like brunch, and finds herself needing to wail the phrase, "I have nothing to wear!" Ew, I just shuddered. Anyway, the chic girl who chooses to go down this rocky road is playing on her deepest fears. Very strategic, as we are all aware that fear is the best motivator. I mean, who wants to walk around with a muffin top or in last season's offerings? I think I'm going to vomit.

The chic girl is always one step ahead of the monster deep within who urges her to make terrible dietary decisions. So while a girl who has stretchy jeggings at her disposal might agree to a donut tour of Brooklyn, the chic girl would never. I mean, who needs a blood orange donut when you have a really tiny MSGM blouse with your name on it? Um, that girl over there in the poly-cotton blend muumuu, apparently.

So, yea. Those J Brand jeans are really cute. You should totally just buy them in a size 24. What do you mean they won't fit? Um, you can lose weight and squeeze into them. They'll look, like, a million times better that way. They can be your reward! Ooh, and that Matthew Williamson top in XS, too. And those really cute Lanvin flats in a size 36. What do you mean those are too small? Um, feet shrink when you lose weight, duh. Anyway, there you go! Celebratory outfit! And who said that weight loss can't be fun?

I'M PRETTY SURE THAT'S ILLEGAL

Cocaine

Oh, blow. Every chic girl will say that she's *over* you, or that she only hangs around you so that she can drink more. "I just really like the smell of it!" chic girl will cry out in protest when confronted about her addiction to you. Yea, whatever. We all know that girls in New York are fucking obsessed with you and want to have a good-sized amount of your kind safely tucked away in the inner compartments of their shiny PS11s at all times.

It's undeniable that chic girls love coke. Not only does it help them to feel prettier and more sparkly, it zaps away any trace of an appetite. It's as if stomachs don't even exist, other than for serving as alcohol-catching receptacles. Plus, chic girls feel totes amaze when it's snowing. Insecurity? Um, bye. Social anxiety? Uh, no. Fatigue? Wait, when were they even tired?

Sure, they'll talk out of their asses and annoy the shit out of passersby, but who cares? So what if they can't move their jaws the next day, or feel as if they went on a 17-mile walk in the Sahara Desert? It's called Gatorade, babe. And that all-consuming nervous breakdown that rears its ugly head as the supply whittles down? Um, that's why they incessantly harass everyone around them for more, duh.

Anyway, I really suggest that you do not dabble in this illicit street glitter if at all possible. It can, like, totally ruin your life! Take my completely insane roommate, Sydney, for example. I mean, she always brags about how she *likes* the drip and I think that she's actually gone three straight days without food or sleep with the help of a big ol' bag of white. She really needs to be on an episode of *Intervention* for her nose problem. She does it all the live long day, be it at work or at the club, and is *so* annoying when she starts giggling and holding hands with random strangers while cooing out that they're, like, best friends. Um, that girl is wearing a dress from *Abercrombie & Fitch*. She is *not* your friend.

But if you choose to do it, boo on you. Just don't be that girl who runs into the bathroom with three of her closest friends and shuts the place down for half an hour. Like, the rest of us actually have to use the toilet, or at least go into the safety of the stall to readjust our Spanx, you nostril scarred betch. Cutting up lines in public restrooms is so tacky, not to mention filthy. What if you get gonorrhea of the nose? That is *so* not cute.

Some chic girls might try to demurely decline when first offered a bump, but everyone knows that they're eventually going to be up doing lines off of hedge fund analysts' stomachs until the wee hours of the morning. But do you really want to be *that* girl leaving the club with raccoon eyes and coke breath, holding the hand of a hastily made decision? Stick to the Adderall, doll.

MDMA

Apparently it's the 90's again, what with the omnipresence of molly and ecstasy, um, every time you open your fucking eyes. Pills such as these make you forget that you know how to do this thing called eating, or about the existence of this thing called food. Unfortunately, it also erases from your mind the existence of these other things known as boundaries, social etiquette and composure.

"Do you want gum?" the chic girl will ask with deranged bush baby-esque eyes as she chews up her entire mouth. "Ohmigod, gum," the fratty, tribal tattoo-ed investment banker bro in the brightly colored tank top will reply as his eyeballs shake violently. "These are, like, my favorite!" she will exclaim as she flips her sweaty mop of wild, tangled hair and they proceed to bond over a package of Ice Breakers peppermint Ice Cubes.

"Ohmigod, I feel like the music is, like, painting itself," the chic girl will comment breathlessly as she's rolling balls. "Like, the music is in color! I can, like, totally see it! It's so pretty! Do you know what I'm trying to say?" The commodities trader in the mirror-lensed RetroSuperFutures will slowly nod as his brain begins to process this transcendental observation, his mouth slightly agape at the genius of it all. "Exactly."

I mean, I can totally see the appeal. Your metabolism skyrockets like cray as your internal body temperature reaches 300 degrees Fahrenheit and you dance the night away. Think of all of the fat globules you're melting off! Everyone also becomes super philosophical and aware of their surroundings. Like, all of the lights are *so* pretty, and why did you never notice them before? That water tastes *amazing*; it must be from, like, France. Plus, everyone is *super* nice, and you think that guy is really cute! And that guy! And that one too! And his friend next to him also!

Although you may burn hundreds of calories while consuming none, you're also bleeding out dignity and grace. Do you really want to be the kind of girl who chews up pills while bobbing along incoherently to some Euro DJ at a crowded afterhours on a Tuesday night in the Meatpacking? Or Electric Zoo? Ew. I mean, you're not in high school anymore.

So if you want to end the night having given away all three packs of your Newport Lights with a busted jaw and your hands covered in someone else's perspiration, be my guest. You'll probably be really gaunt and super hydrated, especially since you hoarded the *entire* water supply, you greedy betch. Like, you might actually look really good after a sanitizing shower and a 14-hour nap. But don't act all aghast when one of your new friends tags you in a photo on Facebook in which you apparently possess glowing orbs for eyes and are immersed in a throng of profusely sweating bros. It just comes with the territory, didn't you know?

Valley of the Dolls

Every chic girl has watched this campy cult classic in her youth and has let out a whimsical sigh while hoping that, one day, she too could be as fabulously chic as Anne, or maybe even Jennifer. Unfortunately, we're all pretty much different variations of the raspy-voiced mess that is Neely, that crazy broad. Like, I'm pretty sure that we've all had drug-induced meltdowns in our underwear. What can we say? We sure do love them booze and pills!

Painkillers, while still technically legal, are basically really convenient doses of heroin. They make you feel fuzzy and pleasant, offering a high that makes you forget about worries, stress and, most importantly, food. You'll completely lose interest in ordering in from Seamless faster than you can say “cold water extraction”. Lights are brighter and everything seems so tranquil when you've taken a Roxy or two. A pair of Percocets makes you feel as if a friendly bear is enveloping you in a warm, cuddly, 4-hour long hug while you ride through the skies together on a fluffy cloud. Your skin will tingle lightly as a light buzzing fills your ears after knocking down some Vicodin. You feel *good.*

Benzos are also uber popular, especially since 99% of chic girls have been prescribed one or another by their concerned psychiatrists. Xanax packs a punch and will make you feel like you're melting into yourself. If you've been prescribed bars of Xanny, your doctor probably thinks you're a hot mess on the verge of a breakdown. Glamorous! Many girls just *adore* Klonopin and Ativan since they can turn you into really chic zombies without rendering your limbs useless. They'll just chill you out and you will look at food and be like, "Oh, hm, there's a croissant. That's cool. Wait, what was I thinking about again? I feel like I was supposed to do something. Huh. Oh well. Whatever." MEN WILL LOVE YOU.

Some weirdos have ravenous appetites on benzodiazepines, but I think that's because they're not inherently chic. Like, everyone knows that anxiety is at the root of chic girls' body dysmorphic disorders and terrible relationships with food. Knock out the crippling anxiousness and you're left with a normal human being who is just really apathetic about everything, including carbs. Yay! Just don't let indifference morph into acceptance. Simple carbohydrates are *never* okay.

Muscle relaxants, à la Soma and Valium, are good for reducing food intake as well. They don't actually do anything to affect your appetite, but they do make you too lazy to even consider moving a finger. The daunting task of walking over to the kitchen to acquire food won't make sense to you in the slightest. Why would anyone want to get up when watching reruns of *Gallery Girls* on the sofa feels *so* good?

No matter what your choice of medication may be, use any

type of prescription tablet responsibly. It is extra chic if you toss it back with some Pellegrino. Just don't get all crazy and chop shit up to snort or freebase or whatever. You are not one of those raggedy club kids who do bumps of K off of the backs of their hands while mascara runs down their faces. You're a lady!

And don't get addicted. Post-rehab weight gain is *the worst.*

BANNED DIET PILLS

“You take one orange and one yellow,” the chic girl will say with an encouraging smile as she rattles the bottles of Brazilian diet pills in her friends' eager faces. “And then you just don't eat,” she will finish with a well-there-you-have-it shrug.

“What's it called again?” her 2 lb-overweight friend will ask with ravenous eyes, scrambling to open the Notes app in her phone.

The chic girl will look at her friend with an annoyed frown and let out a sigh. “I don't know. It's in, like, Brazilian. I can't pronounce it!”

“Portuguese,” the annoyingly intellectual friend will correct her with a sniff.

“Um, they're from *Brazil,*” chic girl will reply slowly with a patronizing smile. “I'm not an astrologist, but that's *pretty* far from Portugal.”

Smarty pants will merely acquiesce with a shake of her head. “Anyway, those can't possibly be good for you. What's even in them?”

"Magic!" the chic girl will breathe out with dreamy eyes.

There's a reason that America is ridiculed for being the land of the obese—our government is being *totally* unfair about weight loss supplements! Anything good is immediately banned, like poor little Phentermine or the super innocent Ephedra. And everything worthwhile is, like, tightly regulated. Um, Pharmacist man, I don't need a twenty-minute lecture on all of the laws regarding Adderall! Trust me, I ain't sharing that shit with *nobody*.

Anyway, you can still get your hands on diet pills from other more forward-thinking countries like Brazil, China and Japan. I tried a few and they feel like Adderall on 'roids. I even, like, fainted a few times from standing up too fast. Your mouth is just parched and you're on fire! In the end, I couldn't handle the mood swings and heart palpitations, though, but some bitches seem to be able to just charge on through. God, I wish I could be *that* chic.

Then there's Clenbuterol. I think it's like asthma medication for horses, but it doesn't come in a giant nerdy inhaler, thank God. Its usage is totally banned by the International Olympic Committee, which must mean that it is super effective in doing whatever it needs to do for Olympic-level athletes. It supposedly speeds up metabolism and messes around with body composition. Basically, the fat gallops straight off of your body and all you're left with is muscle. *So* tempting, I *know*.

FODDER FOR YOUR SHRINK

Competition

When all else fails, take a good hard look at your skinniest friend. Why aren't you skinnier than her? Ohmigod, *all* the boys are, like, totally enamored with her collarbones. That bitch's arms look better in that Wang tee, too. Time for some good ol' jealousy, the greatest motivation, like, *ever*.

Chic girls are *all* about comparing, contrasting and delivering backhanded compliments. "You look healthy," one will say while giving her friend who gained 3 pounds the once-over. The annoying girl with the totally unfair, lightning-fast metabolism is usually on the receiving end of a borderline-hostile "I wish *I* could eat bialys without caring." Such is the world of chicness, but use it to your advantage and you will reap nothing but rewards.

How does she stay so skinny? This is the time to make keen observations and adjustments to your own diet. If she indulges in a glass of wine, drink half. When she nibbles on a chunk of cheese, have a grape. And if she consumes but a few leaves of spinach from her locally-foraged salad, feast on some air. Your hips will thank you.

Once you are the skinnier one, she will immediately take notice and reciprocate accordingly. This literal *Hunger Games* of sorts will continue until both of you reach a BMI of 16, at which it will end abruptly. "Ohmigod, you look *so* good," you will tell her as she honestly replies, "No, *you* look so good!" Bones will clank together as the two of you link arms and embark on an impromptu shopping trip to spend all of the money saved by eschewing food on size 24 Rag & Bone jeans.

An army of skinny waifs is always chicer than just one, didn't you know?

MODERATION

My ex-boyfriend was a total waste of the best eight months of my life, but he had the most *amaze* apartment off of Columbus Circle. And anyone with a functional nose who has ventured into the area has likely been caught downwind of the glorious fumes that the ovens at Bouchon Bakery emit. Did you catch a whiff of that? You know what that smell is, right? You guessed it—butter and sorcery.

On the rare days that I shamelessly chose to slip my willpower a Rohypnol, usually after a soul-crushing argument with the aforementioned douche lord, I would traipse into that evil patisserie and take my frustrations out on a Thomas Keller Oreo. I know, I know—I'm grimacing as we speak. But it totally wasn't my fault. Blame the ex-boyf. He had the gall to call me a delusional bobblehead! Um, rude. My head does *not* bobble.

Anyway, chicness is ingrained into your soul and can never be completely abandoned, didn't you know? Even before I handed over my credit card to complete the shameful transaction, I was making deals with myself in exchange for the imminent cookie scarfing that was to take place. Like, if I was going to treat myself to one of those heavenly delights, then I was *so* not going to be allowed to eat for the next 25 hours. Why not 24? Er, because I'm an overachiever, duh.

"Everything in moderation" is a mantra that every chic girl should live by. I mean, temperance is one of the best methods that a chic girl can employ when she simply *must* indulge in that fully loaded White Chocolate Mocha or that Dutch pancake at brunch. It's really unhealthy for your diet if you never allow yourself the occasional treat.

So go ahead and have it! I mean, you haven't allowed yourself a genuine treat since, like, the year 2009! You totally deserve it. Besides, you've been *sooo* good lately!

Be aware, however, that every silver-lined cloud has a big fucking thunderstorm waiting to shoot out of its ass. Like, don't think that you can nonchalantly inhale a curry donut and then proceed on with life as if some maje caloric depravity hadn't just occurred. Um, no, bitch.

You better brace yourself for the restriction and suffering that is totes necessary for bringing your overall caloric intake back into an acceptable range. Remember, you can't have your cake *and* eat it too. Well, I mean, you totally can. Just don't expect to be able to enjoy life for the next day or so.

Compromise

“I have $17 in cash. Maybe we can do ramen at Totto? Ooh, or should I go buy a new Chubby Stick? I'm also thinking of trying, like, a really red lip. Which one is the shade that Rihanna always wears? MAC Ruby Woo? Yes or no? Yes or no? Feeling kind of dramatic lately,” the chic girl will contemplate aloud to her blatantly anorexic co-worker, Becky, come lunchtime. “Food or beauty? Come on, Becks. Food? Beauty? Er, dilemma!”

“I don't think we should eat,” Becky will quickly reply with rabid eyes. “Yes, we really shouldn't.”

“Are you sure? I'm kind of craving something really bad and carb-y,” chic girl will whimper as she picks up her really cute I-work-in-an-office-and-totally-needed-an-appropriate-satchel PS1 bag and begins walking toward the door.

“We should totally just go to Sephora,” Becky will spit out with a crafty smile on her face. “Food is a complete and utter waste of money!” she will add in a shrill voice.

“Ohmigod, you're right,” chic girl will agree with an incredulous smile on her face. “Thanks for stopping me. I can't believe I was being so cray for a second there.”

"Yes, totally crazy," Becky will affirm as she continues to mumble to herself. "Totally. Crazy."

Did you know that if you forgo buying lunch for a week, you're already halfway on your way to a new Mulberry keychain? Or that if you don't splurge on sushi dinners for a month, you could possibly buy yourself a new pair of Lanvin flats? And, like, you know what's even better for both your wallet *and* your diet than that $12 green juice? That's right—water fast!

Every chic girl knows what it's like to check her credit card balance and be like, "Ohmigod, did someone steal my identity? Why is this so, like, high?" She will scramble to load her recent transactions with a hopeful feeling in her tiny gut, only to be met with a totally upsetting backlog of absurd charges at Whole Foods and Juice Press.

Er, did she really need that $13 pile of soggy kale? Or those $3 avocados? Why the hell had she spent $25 on a jar of Manuka honey? And what was she *thinking* spending $15 on a palm-sized wedge of Apricot Stilton cheese? Ugh, doesn't she know that fancy food just ends up in the sewer with the digested runoff of McDonald's double cheeseburgers and greasy slices from Totonno's? Like, can she pet that grilled radicchio salad lovingly or get major compliments on her bowl of organic carrot ginger soup?

I didn't think so.

"Ohmigod, I could have bought a Rodarte sweatshirt if I didn't do that damn juice cleanse with Melissa," she will wail miserably as she throws her phone against the wall and chews up a Klonopin. "And I only lost, like, two fucking pounds!"

Peer pressure sucks, I know. Just because your supposed friend can convince her sugar daddy to shell out a couple hundred bucks for a barrel of ephemeral liquid feasting doesn't mean that you should have to pour your money into the cold-press juicer, too. Like, the only peer whose pressure you should succumb to is Becky. Bitch obvi knows what she's doing.

So the next time that you're considering forfeiting a small fortune for one day's worth of macerated cucumbers and kale droppings, think twice. You could totally buy a super sleek Feu de Bois candle from Diptyque for the same amount. I mean, one day is extremely short-lived, after all. But do you know how long an exorbitantly priced candle can burn? 150 chicly-scented hours.

While the word "compromise" may not exist in the chic girl's everyday lexicon, like when it comes to what her significant other wants, she should really learn to adopt it when it comes to food. Like, is she really that hungry? Does she *really* need that quinoa salad? Um, no. But does she have an undying need for those go-with-everything Marni slingback wedge sandals? Yes. Yes, she does.

Lying

"You guys go ahead," chic girl will tell her friends with an encouraging smile. "I'm *so* full. I totally gorged on my leftovers from lunch right before I got here."

Of course, chic girl isn't a complete and utter Pinocchio. She really *did* stuff herself with the remnants of her noon-time meal on her way to a late dinner with the girls. But does she really have to explain to them that all she had mid-day was a giant bowl of oxygen with half a pack of Marlboro Lights on the side?

Chic girls are *all* about the "I already ate before I came." Uh-huh, sure you did, betch. That's why your breath smells like Trident and sweet death. Surprisingly, no one ever challenges the utterer of this phrase, even *if* she looks like she is on the verge of anemic collapse. I guess that chic girls are just really ~~gullible~~ ~~ignorant~~ ~~self-absorbed~~ ~~apathetic~~ trusting people.

Her friends will nod understandingly as they pick at their undressed salads and pat the hand of The Girl With No Self Control. They all know where she's coming from—they've all been in that deep, dark place before too.

Or maybe she's so sick, *cough cough*, that she can't muster the energy to go out. Aw, she can faint from hunger in the comfort of her own bed. Or something came up and she can't meet today? Yea, it's called getting a colonic and taking a Percocet to reset her aura. Or she has to go away for the weekend and will make sure to come out next time? Um, hello 48-hour fast!

The only thing is, chic girl has fooled everybody. With her strategic fibbing, she has relieved herself of any obligatory calorie consumption while maintaining a stomach full of air. Of course, she must make sure not to overdo it, so as not to draw attention to the deceitful nature of her carefully fabricated tale. Subtlety is key! So just sit pretty or lock yourself up, and try not to let your stomach grumble too loudly. No one will suspect a thing.

And using this excuse every time you go out will not paint you in a good light, either. You will simply become known as that Charlatan Who Doesn't Eat. And no one wants to be branded an anorexic liar!

Besides, being chic and skinny is supposed to be effortless, didn't you know? *Truly* chic girls are a part of a rare breed of mystical creatures who are magically capable of eating french toast-flavored rice pudding with crumb cake topping all the live long day and *still* weigh in at 89 pounds. They're like fucking nutritional unicorns.

So pick up that spoon, you deceitful little troll, and slowly proceed to advance that glob of sin toward your mouth, stopping *just* as it hovers but half a millimeter away. Then, cry out something like "You guys, is that Jake Gyllenhaal?" or "Look! A three-legged puppy!" as you point across the street. When no one's looking, quickly throw a big portion of that shit into the trashcan, onto the sidewalk or even directly onto an adjacent toddler. Your friends will be none the wiser, and the kid's parents will probably just be like, "Ohmigod, *again*?"

So, like, yea. I can't believe I just inhaled, like, half of this entire bowl. I don't think I can finish it. It's, like, *way* too sweet. And this flavor isn't really what I expected. Or, actually, I'm just super full. Ugh, come to think of it, my stomach doesn't feel all that great. I really shouldn't have eaten that when I'm, like, *so* sensitive to dairy.

Yea, sure, you might be a total Aesop, spewing out folklore and fables about all of the uber fatty things that you supposedly binged on. But, like, who really fucking cares? Be smart about your fibbing, and no one can really disprove you. I mean, they were standing right there the entire time.

"Gawd, you're so lucky. How does you stay *sooo* skinny when you're constantly shoving your face with waffles and all of the amaze lunches that you Instagram?" your jelly friends will ask. "I must just have a really fast metabolism," you can say as you shrug your shoulders. I mean, it's just, like, genetic. Duh.

HISTRIONIC PERSONALITY DISORDER

What kind of girl finds room in her schedule to eat if she's *always* in the spotlight? Being a star is *super* time-consuming, didn't you know? And, I mean, who really needs food when you're feeding off the energy of it all? Being the center of attention is, like, totally satiating on its own. Plus, you don't want to be caught with a mouthful of greens when all eyes are on you. It's just, like, really not an attractive look.

Chic bitches are all about the “Me! Me! Me!” Nobody can seek attention like the chic girl, duh. She's just, like, on the next lev. It's stated on Wikipedia, aka The Encyclopedia of Life, that “people affected by Histrionic Personality Disorder are lively, dramatic, vivacious, enthusiastic, and flirtatious.” Um, yea. I don't see how any of those adjectives are negative. But whatevs. I bet that HPD was just made up by some frumpy psychiatrist who was super jelly of her glittery younger sister who got all of Mommy and Daddy's love. What a freaking betch.

Anyway, Histrionic Personality Disorder sounds *so* misleading. I mean, it sounds like the clinical name for a contagious rash, or something. If anything, this “mental disorder” should be called The Curse of Fabulosity or Super Sparkly Syndrome. Like, have you read the symptoms? They're basically just the guidelines for being really chic. Ooh, The Crazy Cute Condition?

Acting or looking overly seductive

Um, what's wrong with that? Have psychiatrists never heard of feminism? That's really wrong to slut shame girls by labeling them as attention-seeking crazies! It's just, like, really mean.

Being easily influenced by other people

Hello! Have you never met a female? We are *all* about peer pressure and being swayed. It's called marketing! Now where the hell did Becky go?

Being overly concerned with their looks

I'm not even going to dignify this one with a response.

Being overly dramatic and emotional

I'm a really passionate person.

Being overly sensitive to criticism or disapproval

We're just super delicate, GAWD.

Believing that relationships are more intimate than they really are

It's not *my* fault that all of the males I encounter are missing their sensitivity chips. Plus, Ben was *totally* brainwashed by his stupid friends. And Jeff just didn't know how to commit!

Blaming failure or disappointment on others

But it's never my fault?

Constantly seeking reassurance or approval

Is it *such* a sin to get a second opinion?

Needing to be the center of attention

Some girls are just born with glitter in their veins.

Be it by throwing a temper tantrum or a pity party, the chic girl knows how to draw eyes to the performance on display. And if you were lucky enough to be born a star, you will likely be labelled as having this supposed “disorder”. Whatever. Wear it like a fucking crown. The bland wallflowers on the sidelines will hiss and jeer, but who cares? Their milkshakes don't bring anybody to the fucking yard, am I right?

Speaking of milkshakes, don't. Just don't. Having a nasty case of Histrionic Personality Disorder is only acceptable if you look the part, if you catch my Marc Jacobs Daisy-scented drift. Like I said, you really shouldn't be calling attention to yourself if you're just going to put on a pie-eating contest for the viewers. Real life isn't an episode of *Diners, Drive-Ins and Dives*.

BEING A TOTAL BITCH

Scowling burns more calories than smiling due to the fact that you actively have to work your facial muscles to express distaste or disapproval. Like, haven't you noticed that a lot of fat people are actually really happy and chirpy? Conversely, a lot of skinny girls are super upset all of the time. Correlation? Er, duh.

After you get into a fight with your boyfriend and cry hysterically for an hour or two, don't you notice that your abs, like, really hurt? It's from all of the muscle twitching that occurred while you were gasping for air and sighing dramatically. I mean, you basically did, like, 500 really unhappy stomach crunches. Plus, I bet that you burned extra calories while producing all of those tears and blowing your nose. Hyperventilating totally speeds up your heart rate too. Ooh, metabolism boost!

And when you're feeling really bitchy and throw shit all over the room, don't you feel the burn in your arms? Especially when you picked up that pile of European fashion magazines and slammed them into the ground for dramatic effect. You might as well have done five reps of ten with 7-pound weights. Go you!

Yelling and scoffing condescendingly are also really great for burning calories. Exercise those pectoral muscles, you cray betch!

Wave your arms and throw your hands in the air in disbelief for maximal calorie expenditure. Stomping around angrily works too! Full body workout, anyone? If you're really into High Intensity Interval Training, you can incorporate intermittent periods of quiet listening into furious bouts of heated argumentation. Can't you just feel the fat melting off?

Being so pissed that you don't even want to leave your bedroom works wonders for your waistline, as well. “I can't even *look* at food right now, I'm so upset” or “get that fucking pizza away from me before I scratch you in the face” are also really effective in getting your point across and keeping your measurements in check.

So the next time that someone has the gall to ask you why you're being such a bitch, merely embrace the opportunity for a good workout with open, flailing arms. They'll be a lot skinnier after you're done and you'll seem really aloof and glamorous afterward. Unhappiness is just, like, really trendy right now. I mean, have you ever seen Annie Wintour or Vicky Beckham crack a smile? But have you seen their arms? Exactly.

Stressorexia

"I'm, like, so busy that I can't even find the time to eat," chic girl will whimper to her friends as she wraps her slightly loose Helmut Lang sweater around her frail body, feigning concern as if she is even slightly upset by this fact. "Like, I totally forgot to eat lunch today. Isn't that sad?"

"You're so lucky," her slightly chubby gal pal, Amy, will whisper enviously.

"Ohmigod, how is that lucky? I'm *so* stressed. I was at work for, like, 60 hours this week. Gawd, you're so insensitive, Amy," she will snap back while beaming proudly on the inside. I'm, like, *so* lucky, she will think to herself as she glares daggers at poor, not-so-little Amy.

Who knew that a steady diet of soy cappuccinos and a palmful of Klonopin was so effective for whittling down to sample size? Well, everybody, I guess. Anyway, who cares if the actual reason that she was glued to her cubicle was because she was scrolling through fashion blogs and thinspo on Tumblr? Obvi it's working!

Being so stressed and busy that you never found the time to

eat is a great excuse for eliminating mid-day calorie ingestion. So go ahead and stress yourself out over trivial matters that are actually not stressful at all. Your collarbones will become razor sharp and your upper arms will soon rival those of an 11-year old boy, just like on fuckyeahthighgaps.tumblr.com.

If meal-skipping were an Olympic sport, you know that the winner of the gold medal would be donning a perf blowout and super sick Saint Laurent boots. Training to be a food-forgoing champion is a super daunting task, but it's made a lot easier when you're preoccupied with other activities, like working long hours or procrastinating. I mean, who knew that you could spend two hours picking at your split ends? What the fuck, it's 5:00 PM already? Ugh, you have to work overtime *again*? Life is just *so* unfair.

All That Other Cray Shit

Occasional Vomiting

Just because you throw up your food from time to time *doesn't* mean that you have a full-blown Renfrew Center-worthy eating disorder. I mean, most chic girls are at least a little bit bulimic, didn't you know? But it's not like they throw up *every* single meal—just effortless things, like ice cream with diet Sprite.

Even my roommate, Sydney, as eerily disciplined as she is, has her occasional moments of weakness. "Let's go get gelato," she will suddenly turn and say to me in a zombie-esque voice on random days. "Er, okay," I will acquiesce cautiously, unsure of why this ano betch wants me to accompany her to pick up tubs of fatty frozen deliciousness. I'm frightened, I will think to myself as she forces me to speed walk with her down Bowery. This does not feel right.

I will stand aside, my mouth slightly agape, as I watch her ravenously order $30 worth of chestnut honey, mascarpone and cinnamon decadance in a hollow voice with empty eyes. I debate with myself as to if I should get a small order of sesame before talking myself out of it. Don't do it, I tell myself sternly. You can buy one-third of a year's subscription to CR Fashion Book instead.

As the boy at the counter passes her the shameful bag full of caloric despair, I fear that my roommate's frail arms will snap in half. She grabs for it greedily and I feel uneasiness in the pit of my [petite] stomach once again. Alas, we make it home safely, her limbs still intact.

I will watch as she rips off the lid of the first plastic container and digs into the slightly melted heap of velvety cream with a big metal spoon that she has procured from the kitchen. Apparently, the adorable yet tiny plastic spoon-thingy provided by the gelateria did not suffice. Crazed bitch does not offer any to me. Rude. I huffily turn on the TV and become engrossed in an episode of *The Rachel Zoe Project*. I want Sky's closet, I decide enviously. Menswear is *so* in right now.

During a commercial break, I look over to glance at the frozen debauchery taking place on the floor next to me. I see Sydney refilling the now-empty plastic container with the murky contents of her stomach. She guzzles down some Gerolsteiner to assist with her extrusion. Once the plastic box is filled to the brim, she carefully walks it over to the bathroom and I hear the toilet flush. But of course. I am not surprised. It's like fucking deja vu.

Life can't just be about all work and no play. Chic girls need their cheat days too, you know? We just handle the aftermath a lot better. I mean, could you *imagine* what would happen if we actually *allowed* that entire half-pint of Half Baked to reach our intestines? Hell no, my body ain't absorbing that shit. I'm really sensitive to dairy!

Of course, vomming doesn't work so well with really carb-y foods like bread or pizza. Once those hit your stomach, the acid comes gushing out, apparently. And, like, tooth enamel erosion is really not cute. Have you *seen* the scary pamphlets about bulimia? Eep! I'd like to keep my teeth, thank you very much. Which leads me to...

Chew-and-Spit

When my friend, Melissa, convinced me to do a wintertime juice cleanse with her, she was *obsessed* with chewing and spitting. “I could cleanse forever!” she would announce as she gnawed on an entire to-go order of lobster fries, which she then proceeded to spit out into a wrinkled Duane Reade shopping bag containing the masticated remains of a roast beef and Cheez Whiz sandwich.

“Why do people complain about juicing so much?” she would ask while dribbling the macerated remnants of a yakisoba hot dog into the kitchen trash. “It's so easy!”

Over the course of four days, I watched her devour and expel an entire 14-inch cheese pizza, a stack of chocolate chip pancakes, five giant Black and White cookies, three cactus tacos, a box of Reese's Pieces cereal, two skirt steak empanadas, a sack of candied nuts, a Starbuck's marshmallow square and two bags of Pirate's Booty. And I wasn't even with her the entire time.

While Melissa's pseudo-binge only occurred due to extenuating circumstances, I know some girls who employ this tactic on the daily. Like, some of my friends spend hundreds of dollars on gourmet snacks from Dean & Deluca, only to send the chewed up mush down the chute in a warm, lumpy gallon-sized Ziploc bag a mere hour later. Perhaps they just want to be fancy about it? I still don't think that a $20 pile of raspberry rugelach deserves to be coughed up, no matter how chic the spitter is. Gawd, they might as well be throwing a pair of Celine creepers into the trash. So wasteful.

Anyway, I don't know *why* Miranda was so shocked and offended in that episode of Sex and the City when her L.A.-based friend demurely spat his steak out into his napkin. Um, you might have moved to Brooklyn, Gingey, but you lived in Manhattan forevs and you went to fucking *Harvard.* Don't try to act like you've never encountered an eating disorder before. You're friends with Carrie and fucking *Charlotte*. You're not fooling anybody!

So while I can't bring myself to blow $50 on untangible pre-vomit, I can see the appeal. It's technically *not* bulimia. Or at least I think it's not. Is it? Whatever. At least your teeth will be safe. Just don't swallow! I mean, *that's* the *real* eating disorder right? And no one likes a binge eater, *especially* herself. Self-loathing isn't a pretty look.

Hypnosis

I am, like, such a good chic guru that I went ahead and tested this out for my swanky brethren. I had only heard about it on Dr. Oz, and we all know that he knows *everything*. Anyway, this isn't that "you are getting very sleepy" kind of shit, which actually made me really sad. I went to my appointment expecting a gypsy or a warlock to greet me at the door of an *I Dream of Jeannie*-esque Moroccan-chic hypnotherapy lair. Sadly, I was met at the entrance of a boring Midtown office by an overenthusiastic middle-aged man with a receding hairline. Um, already mentally drafting my "I demand a refund" e-mail.

"I have issues with binge eating, over eating, not exercising and craving terrible food," I lie to him. "So please fix all of them, thanks."

"Of course! Please! Lay down on the sofa and relax! We will get started right away! I can definitely help you with those issues!" he screams at me.

"Um, okay," I mumble as I perch warily on the faux-leather chaise lounge. Gawd, I hope he doesn't take advantage of me while I'm sedated like that dentist on *Nightline*, I fret to myself. He totally looks like he has a listing in the sex offender's registry.

"Now! Imagine! Your body is getting heavy!" he begins enthusiastically. "Your arms! They're getting heavy! And then your legs! Down to your toes! All of your limbs are becoming heavy and slack! Heavy and slack! You're so heavy that you can't even bear to fight it!"

"I'm not heavy," I grumble to myself, slightly offended by this rude insinuation as I try to focus.

"Your lids are getting heavy! Let your entire body relax!" He turns on a weird sleep sound machine track as he continues to yell at me to let go of the tension in my muscles.

The Valium that I took on my walk to the office starts to kick in and I feel my body sinking into the hard fake leather surface of the chaise. Ooh, this should start getting good.

"You will make healthier choices!" the hypnotherapist cries out. "Food is not your enemy! You do not need to destroy it! Food is your friend! It is nourishing! It gives you energy and health! Embrace a healthy relationship with food! Eat to live! Don't live to eat! You will eat many small meals every day! You will no longer eat until the food is all gone! You will only eat until you are full!"

"Wait a minute," I try to call out in protest, but my vocal muscles have relaxed into oblivion. Fuck, maybe I should have eaten something before taking my pill.

"You will listen to your body and eat when you are hungry!" he begins again.

"Oh, fuck," I manage to mumble as I doze in and out of sleep. "Stop."

"You will eat what you crave but stop when you are full! Cravings arise when your body is trying to tell you it needs something!"

"Ohmigod, stop," I attempt again as I try to lift myself up.

"Relax!" he screeches out at me.

"This is counterproductive," I murmur as I swing myself upright and begin ambling towards the door. "You're going to ruin me, fake warlock."

"I don't give refunds!" he calls out after me.

"Fucking keep it," I grumble as I run away from the destructive Jedi Mind Control as fast as I can. Good riddance!

And there you have it. I almost commited dietary suicide by allowing someone to instill insane verbal voodoo into my carefully curated thought processes. So unless you can find someone who is willing to actually *help* you, I don't suggest this method of weight loss. It can really undo years of hard work and self-manipulation! I mean, maybe if you *do* have binge eating issues, or whatever, then it would work. But for the *truly* chic, stick to your own mind games. At least the tiny voice inside of your head is a skinny little bitch.

THINSPIRATION

“Sweat is just fat crying”

“Do not reward yourself with food—you're not a dog”

“Nothing tastes as good as being skinny feels”

“Do it for the thigh gap”

“Coffee, smokes and cold Diet Cokes”

“Hip bones and collarbones”

“Eating isn't very Chanel”

Ohmigod, reblog, right? Every chic girl, no matter what her age, is obsessed with thinspo and fucking eats that shit for dinner. It's super satiating. There's a different type of thinspiration or fitspiration for whatever kind of mood you might be in, too. Those 13-year olds on Tumblr have really got you covered.

Feeling lazy? Go read some ridiculous inspirational quotes about “doing today what you won't regret in one year”. Er, guess I should go for a run now. Feeling hopeless? #Beforeandafter! Feeling ravenous? Go on an infinite scroll-fueled journey through a neverending compendium of candid photos of runway models. Ooh, Frida looks super skinny there. Gawd, look at Anja's hips. Abbey Lee's cheekbones—I *die*. And Vlada's clavicles? So jelly.

When you are really unable to drown out the annoying bitch that is your empty stomach, head for the darker side of thinspo. All of those angled shots of thigh gaps and artsy snaps of ribcages are really effective for quelling your appetite and making you hate yourself. These girls mean serious business. Gawd, I wish I had that kind of dedication.

Ooh, that one's kind of extreme. Like, I can literally see her bones, and *not* in the good way. Holy shit, her spine is like that of a fucking Stegosaurus. And, whoa, let's scroll past these uber quickly. Um, are *those* types of GIFs even allowed? They're kinda porn-y. Okay, now *that's* just porn.

Uh, I didn't really need to see your Post-Impressionist suicide collage note, *spiraling-down-to-85lb*, whoever the hell you are. Talk about sadsies. Er, what's with the razorblades? No, don't do that! Ohmigod, why are people taking pictures of blood? Is that a dead person?! Um, close window.

Ugh, now I really need a Xanax. *So* upsetting.

...But those shoulder blades that I just reblogged are *totally* my thinspiration. Ooh, let's go look at the tags for Alexa Chung and Snejana Onopka. Ohmigod, this blog is totes amaze—follow! And, like, did you see that picture of that girl's legs in those adorable knee-high socks? Gawd, I'm *such* a heifer. Time for a 5-day water fast!

Public Eating

"You guys, I was *such* a cow today," chic girl will cry out theatrically with a faux hint of despair in her voice. "I've just been so bad lately! Don't let me have anything other than three pieces of crudité, okay? You're all on Whale Patrol."

By publicly decrying her supposed binge earlier that day, a chic girl can get away with eating but a few paltry stalks of asparagus or a few bits of cheese. Fussing about how much she ate before she arrived at Destination B is somewhat of a habit for the chic girl, as has been previously discussed when mentioning her penchant for concocting tales of The Lunch That Never Was. But by acting as if she actually *wants* to eat, and then performing the godforsaken act, she totally dispells any presumptuous suspicions that she is one of *those* girls who intentionally starves herself. But look at her! She looks so pained as she nibbles on that piece of super yummy bruschetta—she must *really* be full.

Many girls will secretly fast and eat only when they are under the scrutinizing eyes of others. That way, when people are like, "Ohmigod, she got sooo skinny. I bet she is totally ano," observant witnesses can be like, "Nuh-uh. I saw her inhale a Cronut the other day. She's totally eating!"

I mean, it only happened if there's proof, right? Like, no one will be in the know about how you scarfed down an entire can of baked beans in bed, so what's the point? What a total waste of calories. But by performing the act of legume consumption in public, you'll have people defending you left and right when someone proposes the presence of ~~enviable discipline~~ an eating disorder.

Um, what are you talking about? The only disorder that *she* might have is that she just really loves to eat, obvi.

So keep in mind that your private noshing, or lack thereof, has no public record. As stated by the great philosopher, Tumblr user *thinnythinbones*, "what you eat in private, you wear in public." Um, yea.

Eating in front of others is basically insurance against suspicions of imbalanced eating habits. You *may* become known as that girl who can eat everything she wants and doesn't gain an ounce (so jelly), but it's always better to be her than the girl who doesn't gain an ounce because she has food issues. Just think of it as conspicuous consumption... but with food.

A Picture Says a Thousand Words

Though there are many a chic girl whose Instagram feed may lead you to believe that she is the PR girl for Whole Foods Markets, there are others who utilize the app for, well, deception. This tactic is somewhat of a technological extension of public eating, though far less calories will need to be consumed while the audience base is largely widened. Um, efficient much?

Basically, no piece of junk food will go uncaptured. When a chic girl sees a giant bacon cheeseburger, she just *has* to be snapped with it before returning it to its owner. She will pose giddily with a slice of greasy pizza hovering dangerously close to her mouth, and ask friends to take a picture of her ecstatically licking an ice cream cone. Plus, everyone knows that chic girls love to take selfies. However, just taking pictures of themselves is kind of narcissistic. But with gourmet props? Totally acceptable!

So post up that gluttonous shot of deconstructed veal osso bucco with "om nom nom" as the caption. Upload that snap of the overflowing bread cart with a delusive comment of "mini loaves, i DIE". And feel free to shower your followers with images of oozing molten lava cakes, piles of squid ink pasta and gigantic deep fried sushi rolls with lines such as "fat ass!" or "diet starts tomorrow" attached. They'll never suspect a thing.

"How does she stay so skinny when she eats so much crap?" acquaintances will wonder in annoyance. "Ohmigod, that looks so good!" they will comment when she posts a picture of the lemon ricotta pancakes that she had at brunch. Um, obvi her friends aren't very perceptive. The only thing that she actually consumed was that glass of iced black coffee in the corner, duh.

Like, didn't you notice that models always pose with crepes oozing with Nutella or giant sandwiches made with, ugh, oily foccacia? Or how they walk about with cans of full sugar Coca Cola and tote around platters filled with cookies? You didn't think that they actually *ate* those, right? Ohmigod, you are, like, so adorbs. If you had a fan page, I'd totally +1.

But see how you were tricked? That's how easy it is. People will totally believe that you're eating all of this amazing food, when all you're really doing is getting super slim! I mean, what kind of crazy person would order all of that good food just to take pictures? Hm. If only they knew.

Well, everyone in the know is aware that the only things chic girls actually devour with avid voracity are their cigarettes. But the internet doesn't have to know that! All they see is that you had brown butter gnocchi for dinner. And Earl Grey panna cotta for dessert! You naughty girl.

This charade can go on forever, which works for long-term weight loss goals. People will just assume that you are extremely well-fed and have excellent exercise habits to work off all of the calories. You can even post a picture of yourself post-workout for extra credibility. Who knew that technology was so diet-friendly?

And as for those thousand words? They're 333 "I'm totally eating!"s with a "duh" attached at the end.

Sharing is Caring

"Do you want to split the Niçoise salad?" Chic Girl N°.1 will ask Chic Girl N°.2 with a hopeful expression. "I don't think that I can finish a whole one by myself."

"Ohmigod, you totally read my mind," Chic Girl N°.2 will respond with an excited nod. "Why do they have to make them so big? My stomach is, like, really tiny."

"I know, right?" Chic Girl N°.1 will reply with an incredulous smile. "American portion sizes are *so* out-of-whack. Gawd, I wish we were French."

"Ohmigod, yea," Chic Girl N°.2 will sigh in exasperation. "Like, did you hear about their Air Diet?"

While splitting an entree might be considered gauche in some parts of the world, it is totes socially acceptable in chic urban centers. Servers in New York City, in particular, are uber accustomed to waifs dividing a single appetizer plate amongst seven of themselves. They don't even mind when really chic girls order nothing other than a Diet Coke. After all, they're like free decorations for the restaurant.

But chic girls aren't just bifurcating their *frisée aux lardons* to be difficult. No, they're just being really sensitive to the issue of hunger in the world! Talk about social awareness, right? Like, it's just grossly extravagant, not to mention totally ignorant, to order an entire plate of ricotta gnocchi if you're barely going to pick at it. It's also really embarassing when the server asks if there was anything wrong with the meal. "Um, no, it's just that I don't really like to eat" isn't really something that you want to say aloud, you know? But if you split it with a friend? Ohmigod, you might as well be feeding an Ethiopian child.

Wasting food is totally irresponsible, especially since there are, like, so many hungry beings in the world. Plus, compost bins are, like, *so* gross. And you don't want those poor little worms to get fat just because *you* were feeling bloated, do you? That's just really selfish.

But, anyway, splitting dishes is just a part of being a socially responsible member of mankind. Like, you could totally start a nonprofit advocating the implementation of the practice. Gawd, who knew that chic girls could be *such* admirable members of society?

...And, like, all of the calories that you save? Ohmigod, *so* worth the $15 split-plate fee.

Coachella

A cesspool of dirt and dry heat located an hour from L.A. is not really the first place that comes to mind when you think about epicenters of chicness, but the Coachella Valley is just that. Or it is, at least, for one weekend in April. And *only* the first weekend, gawd.

"I'm thinking like a Bohemian Indian war chief with flowers in my hair," chic girl will tell her friends, secretly calling dibs on her fashion theme for the three day-long affair. "But not like a fucking flower crown. I'm talking, like, interwoven tiny flowers with lots of teasing. Ooh, can you take Oribe spray on the plane? Is there a Barney's in Indio?"

Chic girls have worked hard to achieve 5% body fat, and they just want to flaunt it. They might feel like hunger manifested as living, breathing beings, but who cares? They look good. And while they might be really unhappy, they fucking love it when people stare at them or ask to take their pictures. So what better place to prance around in skimpy photogenic outfits than at Coachella?

"Or the whole Native American thing is over, huh? How about a Tibetan wood nymph? Or a dystopian hippie? Do people wear black in California? Are my Balenciaga cutout boots appropriate for the fields? Do you think Tommy Ton will be there?"

In preparation for their weekend of frolicking and debauchery, chic girls will cut out carbs, or even food in general, for the entire month prior. It's basically the same routine that's involved in preparations for Fashion Weeks, but the resulting outfits for which they strive are a lot more revealing. So cut that bowl of broccoli in half, betch, because you *know* you want your arms to be taut as fuck.

While it may be difficult to juice cleanse in March, at least the temperatures are no longer bone-chilling. The chic girl will push on through, as she knows that she will be rewarded with a frail form on which everything looks fabulous. Plus, it's really warm in California, so that's like a reward in and of itself, right?

And when a chic girl finally arrives in the desert after a solid month of preparation? She will prance around for maybe 15 minutes, after which she will whine about the people and the lines and the weather as beads of sweat form atop her brow. The rest of her days will be spent in her hotel room or at fashionable parties located miles away from the fields, only popping onto the festival grounds sporadically when temperatures are manageable. Ohmigod, Grimes and Vampy Weeks, yay.

"It was *so* much fun," she will prattle on to her friends over brunch once she returns. "They had green juice there too! So I basically continued my cleanse all weekend. You guys should really go next year. We should totally do VIP."

Boo, You Whore

Boys are great for a lot of stuff, like buying us drinks, providing air-conditioned enclaves in Soho and putting up with undeserved verbal beatings. Like, who else could calmly endure the epic bitch fits that are thrown simply because you're in a really bad mood? Not your hungry girlfriends, that's for sure.

Though chic girls will try to deny it, boys are also strong motivators for weight loss and dieting. Honestly, they just want to look good so that they can attract ~~rich old guys~~ quality men, didn't you know? Boys will act as if they prefer full-figured (i.e. chubby) betches, but everyone knows that they love thin limbs and svelte stomachs. Um, there's a reason that they eat up the Victoria's Secret Fashion Show every year and not *Here Comes Honey Boo Boo.*

Take, for instance, what one of my super rude but super truthful male acquaintances confided in me before. He literally told me that he likes to take home “sacks of bones”, which is actually kind of derogatory and creepy. But whatever. There you go! Proof positive that boys basically love thinspo too.

Boys in finance and big law are your best bets if you want to avoid the dreaded "love pounds" that are gained during the early phases of a budding romance. These overworked motherfuckers are *way* too busy dealing with laser printers and Powerpoint presentations to whisk you off to dinner or take notice of your abberant eating habits. All they know is that they're dating a super hot betch who is quite vocal about her predilection for NET-A-PORTER.com.

Ooh, he's stuck at the office and needs to cancel dinner *again*? Um, score. You get to extend your water fast by another 12 hours *AND* he's going to get you that Givenchy watch you wanted so you won't throw a shoe at his face like last time? Ohmigod, talk about a dream relationship.

I am not going to delve into the topic of bedroom relations because chic girls are ladies, and speaking on such matters is just *so* not elegant. But let's just say that obvi you can burn a lot of calories by engaging in coital affairs. So if all of the SoulCycle classes for the day are full, you can def seek out a male companion for a good cardio workout if you so please.

Just understand that there is no reason to use a treadmill on one day, an elliptical the next, a rowing machine on Wednesday, a Bosu Ball later that afternoon and then a Stairmaster the next morning. That just makes you a slut. And a girl of a lascivious nature is *not* chic. Just ask my ex-friend, Courtney.

LOVED THE CHIC DIET?
UM, DUH.

You can get updates from all the new releases from the author via

http://www.kitolsen.com
or
http://www.thechicdiet.com

You can also receive news by signing up for her
mailing list on either site.

Be sure to also check out more from the
other ~~betches~~ authors at Wunderland Press!

http://www.wunderlandpress.com

We've even included an excerpt from *Etoile*, a super chic novel about a struggling fashion model looking for love, from rookie author, Olivia Besse.

Talk about generous, am I right?
#Dying!

Etoile (The Mannequin Series, #1)

by
Olivia Besse

One

Elodie stood against the wall, cigarette in hand, posing for the photographer who had stopped her to ask if he could take her picture for his street style blog. She did not see what the big deal was, as she was simply wearing the standard model outfit of boots, skinny jeans, a plain tee shirt and a leather biker jacket. All in black, of course.

“Can I get a close-up of that?” he asked as he gestured to her ring.

“Of course,” Elodie told him with a smile. She knew better than to be flattered by his attention, as everyone knew that street style photographers were the biggest modelizers of all, but she couldn't help but feel giddy that he had stopped to take her picture.

"Excellent. Thank you so much," the blogger smiled at her as he checked the photos on his giant camera. “Here's my card. Be sure to check out my blog! Your post should be up soon.”

She smiled back and took the card nonchalantly, her underwhelmed expression belying the fact that she would probably end up obsessively checking the site on the hour, every hour, to see if her picture had yet been uploaded. Due to the years of relentless bullying, scrutiny, humiliation and criticism that she had endured, she had developed a particularly nasty habit of analyzing every last pixel of any photo in which she had been immortalized.

Of course, her analysis paralysis, as her therapist had termed it, didn't just end there. In spite of the confidence that she worked so desperately to emit, Elodie Marais was a self-deprecating mess. Her past had scarred her to the point of her having anxiety attacks whenever she felt helpless in a situation. From her point of view, the only way that she could avoid being hurt or abandoned again was if she could have complete control over her future.

Any sentence that escaped her lips had thoroughly been repeated in her mind a minimum of ten times, and every chic outfit that she had "just thrown on" had its components carefully curated for hours before she wore them out. She could barely function, let alone relax, without the help of barrels of alcohol and hoards of prescription and illegal drugs.

Tucking the thick square of paper safely into her black Givenchy tote, she proceeded on her way to her photo shoot, which was scheduled to begin in an hour. On her short walk on the tree-lined streets of the West Village, she ignored the sprinkling of tourists in fanny packs who unabashedly snapped her picture with their camera phones and ogled at her statuesque presence.
Did they assume that she was someone famous? It made her sad to think that they were probably just taking pictures of her because she was the first photogenic giant that they had come across on their trip to the big city. They had probably just arrived straight from the airport, she thought to herself as she continued to make her way down the long city block. Didn't they know that towering teenaged girls with swishy hair and pin thin limbs were a dime a dozen in Manhattan? Once they encounter their umpteenth model on the street, they probably won't even give that poor girl a second glance, she grumbled inwardly with a slight shake of her head.

Elodie was now nineteen years old and living in a cramped model apartment in Manhattan. She had officially signed with Groupe Models in London three days after her fifteenth birthday, just in time to debut at the Spring/Summer shows at Milan Fashion Week. She had grown exponentially over that summer like a willow tree, and Janet had personally marched her around the city to local agency offices like a prize doll.

The agency heads, casting directors and bookers had fawned over her like a newborn puppy, grooming and training her to perfection. "Bellissima! Walk like this, gattina," the wrinkled walking coach wearing too many prints and way too much bronzer had directed the lanky girl as she attempted to saunter down a makeshift runway. "You hair is so pretty, dolcezza, I will just give you tiny highlights to make your eyes pop," the flamboyant hairstylist had cooed to her as he smoothed down her locks. "Here's a tip. Whenever you take pictures, make sure to point your chin down slightly. You have such a lovely chin," the agency's photographer had taught her with a warm smile. Elodie had gushed inwardly to herself about how everyone was so kind and helpful. Little did she know that, to them, she was just fresh meat and a new source of revenue to be earned.

They had squealed out odd things that Elodie hadn't understood, such as "she's just like an alien nymph lost in a storybook" or "she looks just like a bewildered Blythe doll, I can't get enough of her". She had a crowd of people surrounding and trailing her at all times with schedules and hairdryers and foundation sponges. In the end, Elodie ended up walking in six big shows, which Janet had said was very good for a new face. And she had been shocked by the resulting paychecks.

Of course, her representative agency in Milan and her mother agency in London took large cuts from all of her earnings, citing outrageous charges for lodging, forwarded allowances for food and her cellular phone, transportation, booking fees, photo retouching and comp card printing. By the time that they were done with her, all that she had to show for countless grueling hours of work were frightening amounts of debt.

Following immediately after the shows in Milan was the notorious Paris Fashion Week. Without so much as one good night's sleep, the young girl was shipped off back to France so that she could stomp down those lucrative runways. As Elodie had not yet begun to show any metabolic slowdown, her waifish figure and French roots were a hit with designers from her motherland, much to the jealousy of her stone-faced competitors.

The wide-eyed child had taken in all of the sights and sounds in wonderment, wanting to take mental snapshots of her first major season. Every intricate detail in the couture shows entranced her, and she always found herself looking around to see if everyone was taking note of all of the amazing things that she was seeing. She watched the seasoned models glumly chain smoke cigarettes, wrinkling her nose at the acrid odor. Why would they smoke those? she had curiously wondered, unaware of the fact that she would one day be smoking upwards of one pack a day.

She shuffled from casting to casting and got barely any sleep during the entirety of her stay, the bags under her eyes expertly camouflaged by strategic applications of concealer and highlighter before the shows. The girl found nary a moment to eat as she was thrust into couture gowns and marched down brightly-lit stages. But who needed food when she was feeding off of the excitement of it all?

After strutting down her last runway, the Valentino Haute Couture show to be exact, an enthusiastic Elodie had pranced into the backstage area in her sneakers and waved goodbye to all of her new friends with a big grin. An older model named Lily had patted her on the head with a sad smile, which had perplexed the then-simpleminded Elodie. What did the beautiful girl have to be so sad about?

Despite her excellent season of walking in seventeen shows and even earning a profile on the New York Magazine Models Directory, she still found that she was left with an exorbitant amount to pay off to her three different agencies. Ever the optimist, the young girl had shrugged the number off, assuming that she would be able to pay it back many-fold in due time. Especially since she was going to be a world-renowned modelling sensation. She was sure of it.

Once her whirlwind stint in Paris was over, she had returned to London to work with Janet, choosing to live in an overpriced model apartment there rather than return to her depressing existence in Châteaudun. Being a dramatic teenager, she had declared that she simply could not bear to return to the small town and face Felix or her obnoxious classmates.

After all, once word had spread when she had first secured her modelling contract, her quiet school life had been flipped upside down. The boys around her would not leave her alone, following her through the hallways and asking her to pose for them.

When she went to the bathroom, she would hear the girls gossip viciously about her while sneaking cigarettes outside of her stall. One of her few former friends, a mousy girl named Berenice, had even started a rumour that Elodie had fabricated the whole story and was actually being sent to Serbia to work on a plum farm.

The day before she was to leave for London, she had heard Marine Villeneuve casually mention to Emmanuelle Thomas that Elodie had the ugliest knees that she had ever seen.

How could a girl become a model with those knees? Marine had demanded loudly while she washed her hands. The cruel girl had then gone on to comment on Elodie's face, stating that she had always thought the model hopeful looked like a cat who had sipped some sour milk. How could Felix have ever liked someone like Elodie Marais, she pondered aloud as Elodie listened from behind the stall door with bated breath.

Emmanuelle had then made a snarky quip that Elodie had probably been wearing pants when the scout had met her. Perhaps even a mask of Kate Moss's face, she had added with a cackle. The two had then left the bathroom in a fit of giggles, the door slamming loudly in their wake.

Elodie remained seated on the toilet seat for the remainder of the day, not bothering to eat lunch or return to her desk. She simply sat on the seat for hours, staring at her wrinkled knees, which she would resent for many years to come, as fat tears dripped onto them. In that moment, she decided that she never wanted to return to her miserable existence in that school. While she had once loved classes and learning, she had grown to resent the lycée and its entire student body as a whole.

And then there had been Felix. He had artfully ignored her for the many months that had passed since that cold winter's day, and Elodie's heart had grown cold towards him. But as she had finally peeled herself from the toilet seat and begun walking home from school at the end of that day, she felt a light tap on her shoulder.

"*Salut*, Elodie," he had said with a tremor in his voice. She had turned around to stare at him with a blank expression as he continued. As he spoke, she felt nothing but a hollow feeling where her heart used to beat warmly whenever he was next to her. Even as he stood but two feet in front of her, his raspy voice sounded as if it were coming from miles away.

He was sorry for having been so distant, he had said, and that he would really like to speak with her after she returned from Milan. She had given him a tight smile and assured him that they would, to which he had nodded excitedly with the grin that used to make her heart flutter.

And with that, she never saw him again.

Janet had proved to be somewhat of a mother figure for Elodie, forcing the young girl to finish her studies online via the CNED so that she could sit for her baccalauréat. "I don't want you to be one of those dumb girls who ruins her future for this," she had said. "You're going to have a degree to your name, or I'm not going to book you for anything!"

So Elodie made her deals with Janet and worked out of London as a real model. She booked fashion and beauty editorials in major magazines and worked hard to build her portfolio and reputation. Elodie was given opportunities that she could have only dreamt of on her tiny little bed in the group home. She modelled couture that cost more than her life, posed with exotic animals in breathtaking locations and travelled all around the Eastern Hemisphere. The Japanese market, in particular, loved her, and she spent three hectic months in Tokyo shooting bubbly commercials and cartoonish beauty campaigns.

After considerable success in Europe and Asia, Janet decided that it was time to let her rising star move on to bigger and better things. So, just as she turned seventeen, Elodie followed Janet's advice and signed to Elle Model Management in New York City, one of the biggest and most prestigious agencies in the world.

In Manhattan, Elodie shuffled endlessly between castings and her model apartment, making few acquaintances other than her handlers and roommates. Many of the other rookie models around her were still fresh and excited, often chirping with each other during the excruciating wait periods before castings. Despite her young age, however, Elodie was already as jaded as a retired movie star.

She often wondered what the other young models were so excited about. Had she ever been that happy and hopeful? A good majority of the new girls, particularly the Americans, were starting their careers out in New York, not having had the extensive experience in the Eastern Hemisphere that Elodie and many of her European counterparts had been given. Thus, they had yet to be ripped apart by casting directors, looted by their agencies, used and abused by the older male models and harassed by smarmy photographers.

They'll see it soon enough, Elodie often thought to herself as she watched the perky bright-eyed girls from Kansas and Missouri chat amiably with each other in the crowded waiting areas. In a few months' time, they won't have anything to smile about either.

Elodie had seen it many times before. So many times, in fact, that it was actually quite humorous, despite the fact that there was nothing funny about it at all. The occasional fifteen-year old rookie would strike it big, causing other genetically-gifted teenagers from around the world to make the costly journey to New York, the mecca for hopeful young models. Fresh-faced girls arrived in droves everyday, each one as determined as the one who came before her. Little did they know that the city and industry would eat them alive so long as they allowed it. She knew the story very well. After all, she had once been one of those starry-eyed girls too.

When she had first arrived, the buzz of the city had given her a new lease on life. She could hardly believe her luck that, at just 17-years old, she was living in the most glamorous city in the world, about to burst onto the scene of the top global modelling market. My whole life is about to change, she remembered thinking as she got out of her first bright yellow New York taxicab. Sure, the driver had smelled like day-old Mexican food and had grumbled acerbically at her, but nothing could have dampened her naive and cheery mood that day.

Walking into the dingy tenement-style accommodations to which she had been assigned didn't faze her. Nor had the detailed list of the agency's endless fees that the bookkeeper had handed to her upon her first visit to the office. Having her new agent, Adam, tell her that she needed to lose five pounds and an inch in her hips merely spurred a feeling of determination within the girl's hopeful little head. She didn't even mind too much when one of the transient roommates took the $60 bottle of Bumble and Bumble hair conditioner from Elodie's luggage as a souvenir on her way back to Germany.

"She must have mistaken it for her own," Elodie had reassured herself aloud as her Texan roommate, Cassandra, rolled her eyes.

It was only after a few weeks that Elodie slowly began to realize the realities of her situation. Watching her roommates eat only the occasional bowl of spinach caused her to start monitoring what she consumed as well. When the other girls went to sit on the fire escape to smoke cigarettes in their pyjamas, Elodie eventually joined them. And when her roommates explained that cocaine worked excellently to quell hunger pains, Elodie was more than happy to partake.

Soon enough, she was the stereotypical chain-smoking model with a permanent scowl affixed on her face. The endless rejections and critiques had hurt her feelings at first, causing her to spend countless nights weeping silently into her pillow. She constantly found herself comparing her body, face and hair to those of every other girl in the room whenever she went to castings. What do they have that I don't? she often wondered with tears in her eyes as she flipped through the glossy advertisements in fashion magazines.

Eventually, she developed a thicker skin that allowed her to shrug off comments about her supposedly uneven shoulders and slightly lopsided lips. Some casting directors said that her calves were too thin, while others said that they had a tad too much muscle tone. Her lashes weren't lush enough for mascara advertisements, and her arms too long for handbag campaigns. She was too blonde, or not blonde enough.

While she had been warmly welcomed by the European and Asian markets, the gatekeepers of New York's modelling bubble always found something scathing to say. Simply put, there were too many girls competing for too few spots, and the margin for error was, essentially, nonexistent.

In a few months' time, Elodie did not give one fuck. In New York City, she was disposable, as there were at least twenty other girls who had the same look with the same imperfectly blonde hair and the same lopsided lips. They were all interchangeable, and nobody ever let them forget that. At times, she felt hopeless, unsure of how she would ever get a chance to show the world what she could do when none of the clients would even give her the opportunity.

When she turned eighteen, she was freed from the confines of her chaperoned dormitory and allowed to move into a smaller apartment with just three other models, all of whom were just as fed up with the industry as she. And, with time, Elodie began doing fairly well for herself.

By the time she turned nineteen, she was booking the occasional editorial or small online campaign. Not much had changed, save for the fact that she had finally learned how to play the game. That is, she had received one vital piece of advice that had become somewhat of a lifeline for her fledgling career.

While working on a job for an old client in Paris right after her eighteenth birthday, a veteran model named Maarja had decided to take the virginal and frustrated Elodie under her wing. Maarja was wildly successful and always had the most beautiful bags and shoes. Elodie yearned to have even half of the success that Maarja had. And one day, Maarja decided to let her in on a little secret.

They had been sitting in their respective chairs after getting their makeup and hair done, waiting for the production intern to call them over to the set. They were shooting an advertisement for a French skincare company's special care line for teenaged skin, and were to play the parts of best friends frolicking through a park in pink dresses, flippy ponytails and deranged smiles.

While they were sitting around until they were needed, Maarja was purring to someone on her phone, making suggestive comments that made Elodie blush.

"Beebi, you are going to buy me La Perla?" she cooed in a high-pitched voice. "You know I only like lace lingerie. Do you not like it too? It is more for you than me, no? Yes, we can do that... Of course, beebi."

After hanging up, Maarja had looked over at the young girl and smiled sumptuously, to which Elodie squeaked out, "Your boyfriend?"

Maarja had looked at her with a bemused smile and replied, "One of them, I suppose you can say."

"You have more than one?" Elodie had choked out with huge eyes. Who was this woman?
As she admired her own reflection in the mirror, Maarja had given the naive girl a sage piece of wisdom.

"Oh, beebi, I am going to help you. You do not have a boyfriend, yes? Good. You are your body. Modelling, it is all about selling your body. Your body gets you power. It gets you money. It is not about who you know, it is about who you fuck. You are just a mannequin. Bat your pretty little eyes and you can have anything you want. Remember that."

And remember she did. On the plane ride home, Elodie thought back on all of her failed auditions and castings. There were always those girls who sparkled, who touched the rare straight casting director or photographer's arm and giggled charmingly. She thought of the many times that she tortured herself by looking at those finished editorials or campaigns that she had been passed up on, only to see that the giggling girls had been chosen instead.

She thought back on how the girls in the images stared back at her with taunting eyes, as if they were part of some secret society to which Elodie didn't belong. How one revered photographer had refused to keep taking test shots of her when she didn't want to take off her shirt, irregardless of the fact that the photos were to be beauty shots of her face. How one of the skinny teenaged models of the moment was well known to be sleeping with the 55-year old head designer of the fashion house that had shot her to fame. How Elodie had none of it, but those minxes had it all.

Sitting in her crappy seat in Economy, she pondered what Maarja had said. It was glaringly obvious that the woman knew what she was doing. The only question was if Elodie was up for the challenge.

All she knew was that she didn't want to live in debt, and she didn't want to wait amongst a sea of girls for her chance at thirty seconds with a photographer who could care less, only to get rejected for the hundredth time. She wanted to be one of those girls in First Class, sipping on champagne and sleeping in her fully reclinable seat. She wanted the money, the fame and the good life. She wanted what she had come to New York for.

In that moment, she vowed to let the frightened child inside of her go. The little brokenhearted girl, what with her emotional scars and low self-esteem, had held her back for long enough. She knew very well what she needed to do, as had the many girls who had come before her.

Taking a deep breath, Elodie swore to herself that she would get as much experience as she possibly could and make it big. Maarja had passed her the golden ticket. This was her chance. She was going to become the best mannequin that she could be.

Want to read more?
Check out the The Mannequin Series,
exclusively on Amazon.com!

21716503R00129

Made in the USA
Middletown, DE
08 July 2015